# WHEN GOD

## *Speaks*

# WHEN GOD

# *Speaks*

# CAN YOU HEAR HIM?

**BY: VALERIE COOPER MIMS**

**Cooper Mims Publishing**
**Baltimore. MD**

First Edition 2016

ISBN-1523751800

Cover Design by Gregory Johnson

Back cover Photograph - Looks By Lloyd Photography

Printed in the United States of America

## TABLE OF CONTENTS

# DEDICATION

This book is dedicated to my wonderful parents, Betty and Chester Cooper, for rearing me in an environment where I learned the importance and power of prayer.

My father has gone home to be with the Lord, but prior to his passing, we talked regularly about the content of this book. He believed in me and encouraged me to finish this book.

To my loving and supportive husband, Angelo; thank you for your prayers and for encouraging me to be all that God has destined me to be.

My husband has gone home to be with the Lord. There are no words to express the magnitude of this loss. Angelo was everything that God commanded a husband and father to be. I will always love him and I hold on to the hope that one day I will see him again.

To my brothers: Anthony Cooper Sr. and Gary Cooper Sr., thanks for always supporting my endeavors and celebrating my accomplishments.

And

Last, but certainly not least, to my precious daughter, Courtney Charde Mims, for being my number one fan. Thank you for using your gift of administration to ensure that this project was completed. You are my earth angel; a true gift from God. I am grateful that God blessed me with you as my daughter.

# ACKNOWLEDGEMENTS

First and foremost, I would like to thank God for birthing this book into my spirit years ago. I am thankful that He entrusted me to complete this project that prayerfully, will encourage and strengthen His people and their relationships with Him. It is my desire that this book will cause His people to pray without ceasing and remain committed to the processes that cause them to hear Him speak.

I am grateful to my pastor, Bishop Walter Scott Thomas Sr., for his leadership and spiritual guidance. It is evident that he is a true man of God who consistently demonstrates his ability to hear when God speaks and carry out His plans.

I am extremely thankful for Minister Elaine Edge for sharing her contacts and experiences as a first time author. Thank you Dr. Pamela Love Manning, book coach, Andrea L. Reid, editor, and Minister Gregory Johnson, graphic designer, for your contributions in making this book a reality.

To my sisters in Christ: Glendell Powell, Barbara Craig, Laura Bailey, Beverly McDermott and Wilma Davis, thank you for covering me in prayer and consistently checking on me throughout the many years of this book's development.

Thank you to all of my colleagues who inspired me to finish this book because they were eager to read it.

## FOREWORD

When God Speaks, Can You Hear Him?" is a provocatively profound description of prayer in action.  Not only is this book inspirational, but it is a phenomenal expression of just how powerful personal prayer can be.. The Author has bared her soul, and was somehow able to translate deep, personal, spiritual experiences into life-changing words on a page.  I was greatly impressed with how smoothly the Author transitioned from the purpose of monologue to the necessity of dialogue with the Master. If you have ever failed to take personal time with God seriously, this book will certainly snap you back into a spiritual reality and relationship through Divine dialogue. From the reading of the first paragraph to the closing sentence, I literally could not put this book down.  And I am sure that anyone who reads this book will share this response.

Rarely is one able to capture the full impact of Divine dialogue and intervention, but this book is an awesome example of just how significant it is to hear every Word from God.  It is comprised of eight thought provoking chapters, each filled with rich personal experiences with the voice of God, as well as practical guidance on how to deepen our connection with the Almighty.  It is ingenious how the Author cleverly weaves numerous personal stories and anecdotes into incredible life lessons.

This book is a must have for any bookshelf.  I believe millions will be helped by this powerful presentation of an awesome, loving, caring, and communicative God.  I have known this Author personally for a number of years, and always recognized the anointing on her life.  But I must say, it is incredible how this Author has transformed life experiences and devotion to God into such a powerful and masterful literary work. If you are serious about hearing God's voice, and desire to go deeper in your communication with God, read this book!


Rev. Dr. Tom A. Bailey, Pastor
Victory Temple Missionary Baptist Church
Alexandria, Virginia

## INTRODUCTION

When God Speaks, Can you hear Him?

When God Speaks, Can you hear Him? is about the power of prayer, the significance of prayer in our lives, and how Satan will do whatever it takes to keep us from praying. We must keep in mind that Satan is the adversary. It is his job to oppose us and all the great things that God has predestined for our lives.

Satan does not want Christians to pray because when we pray, we do damage to his kingdom. When we pray, sickness and diseases are healed, minds are renewed, shackles are loosened, addictions are broken, relationships are restored, burdens are lifted, and broken hearts are mended. When we pray, families are reunited, suicide attempts are interrupted, thought processes are elevated, peace is restored, hope is renewed and our dreams become reality.

Praying allows us to grasp the magnitude of who we really are in Christ. It also allows us to see the power that resides within us. In essence, prayer prepares us for victorious living, spiritual battle and helps us to be successful in every area of our lives.

Now, if you paused right here, and re-read the last two paragraphs, really absorbing and meditating on the life changing effects of prayer, it would become clear to you why Satan does everything in his power to prevent us from praying. He will do anything and will use anybody to keep us distracted, deceived, uninformed and spiritually weak. Who is more cunning, more devious, and more deceiving than Satan? The answer to this question is no one. No one is better at getting us off course and feeding us lies than Satan. He is the enemy and master of lies and deception. He prides himself on distracting us by pulling us away from the things of God.

I am reminded of a song that we use to sing when I was a child entitled, "Satan, we are going to tear your Kingdom Down." Prayer is the most effective tool we can use to demolish Satan's kingdom. If we really took the time to think about the power of prayer and the results it yields, we would pray more often. The cliché, "Prayer changes things" is indeed true. When we pray, God listens and moves on our behalf.

Praying is communicating with God. We are truly blessed to be able to sit down and commune with the Creator of heaven and earth, the Lilly of the valley--the Great I Am. We should never take for granted or under-estimate this great privilege of being able to talk to the Almighty God!

Just the thought of imperfect mortal men having total access to an immortal perfect God, is enough to blow our minds. But thank God, He has made it possible. We really can talk to Him and share the issues that weigh heavily on our hearts and minds. We can place all of our questions, concerns, and burdens in God's lap—and leave them there. One of the greatest rewards of praying is having God to provide us with feedback and strategies on how to handle those things that try to steal our joy and peace.

The goal of this book is to start a war; not a physical war but a spiritual one. I want to wage war on anything and everything contrary to the perfect will of God. I want to reenergize all of God's prayer warriors. I am calling you from the North, South, East and West. I'm seeking prayer warriors who know that God is still in control, and who will fight until lives are changed, souls are saved, and healing and deliverance take place.

I am interested in prayer warriors who have been running for Jesus for a long time and are not tired yet. If you are a prayer warrior or want to become one then keep reading. Perhaps, you are just a babe in Christ and have not yet been convinced of the power of prayer, but somehow you can feel the hand of God and His gentle spirit pulling you closer to Him. This is so that He can reveal the great plans He has for your life. As I said before, prayer is the vehicle that allows us total access to God.

It has been said that the greatest offense is a good defense. My daughter's basketball coach often told her players that offense sells tickets but defense wins games. She told the girls that they were in the game to win! Therefore, she placed great emphasis on teaching the girls defensive moves. She taught them to keep their hands up for the block, to get low for the steal, and keep their feet planted to take the charge. She taught them to get down the court quickly, read the offense in order to determine their defensive formation. They needed to know whether to get in a full court press, a man to man, or a 2-3 zone. She instructed them to keep their eyes on the ball and to stay alert at all times. She instilled in them the ability to be able to hear and decipher the coach's voice in the midst of a screaming crowd. Well my friends, I happen to agree with Courtney's coach. We are in this game called life to win! And if we are going to win, we must learn how to fight defensively. If we learn to identify Satan's tactics and tricks, then we will not fall prey to them. If we take the time to study Satan's moves then we will be able to make counter moves that will defeat him every time.

It is my prayer that this book will compel you to pray. The more you pray, the more your relationship with God is strengthened. As your prayer life increases, a love relationship begins to form. This new love affair with God will cause your heart to flutter just thinking about entering into His presence. This bond is sweeter than the honey in the honeycomb. It will cause you to seek out quality time to be alone with God. Quality time with God has long lasting effects. It equips us to handle life; its ups and downs, its successes and failures, and its appointments and disappointments. Prayer helps us to face our obstacles, conquer our fears and accept the inevitable. Prayer causes us to sing when we should be crying. It causes us to dance when we want to curl up in a corner. Only constant communication with God can help us successfully navigate through life with all of its stressors and unpredictable moments.

And when our prayer shifts, from a monologue (man talking to God) to a dialogue (God and man talking to each other), our lives will never be the same. It is important that we move from a monologue to a dialogue because we cannot tell God anything that He does not already know. In fact, He knew it before we knew it and He knew it was going to happen before it happened. So, if He can patiently listen to us tell Him what He already knows, we surely need to learn to be quiet in order to hear His instructions. Not only can He clarify situations we do not understand, but also those situations we think we understand.

The voice of God is like none other. It is strong, yet gentle; piercing yet comforting; and distant yet present. When God speaks specifically to our situations by giving us clear directions, (via a specific scripture, a special song, the preached word), we instantly feel peace and our burdens are lifted. We are renewed and we know that we can make it because we have heard from God. We can stand confidently knowing that everything will be all right because God has spoken!

# Chapter 1
# *Something to Think About*

# Chapter 1
## *Something to Think About*

Life has taught us how to act when we enter into the presence of greatness. Psychologically, socially and emotionally, we have been trained to expect and accept certain protocols and procedures in specific situations whenever we are privileged to be in the company of important people such as celebrities and dignitaries. When we come into their presence, we usually anticipate that there will be a significant amount of space between us and them. We expect that there will be large crowds, long lines and high security. In most cases, unless invited to the after-party or a smaller, more intimate setting, we do not expect to shake their hands or engage in one-on-one conversations with them. However, despite all of these annoyances and inconveniences, it is amazing to think what we will do, how far we will go, or how much money we will spend, just to be in their presence.

I am reminded of a time when my church, New Psalmist Baptist Church, was privileged to have former President, Bill Clinton, visit our church. The members of my church, and countless others, were excited to be in his presence. Although we may have seen this prestigious individual in the media, it was no comparison to actually seeing him in person. The excitement of his arrival began weeks prior to his coming. There was a great deal of preparation for his visit. Security was at an all-time high. White House security, unbeknownst to the general congregation, visited to ascertain the order of the service, the physical structure of the church, where the president would enter the building, where he would sit, who would sit in the chair next to him, the best time for his entrance into the service once it began, when he would be called to the pulpit, what door he would exit, and on… and on… and on.

Since Bishop Thomas did not publicly announce which service the President would be attending, many members (myself included), showed up for the seven-thirty a.m. service. We thought the President would surely want to get in and get out early, but we were wrong--(No president…No problem). We stayed over for the nine-thirty a.m. service. Yes, we figured this would be the service. If he did not come for the early service, he must be coming to the second service, but we were wrong again--(No president…No problem). We stayed over for the eleven-thirty a.m. service. This was the one! Yes, this was the service we had been waiting for. We really were about to sit in the same room as the President. We were so excited to actually have the opportunity to be in the same Sunday morning worship service with Bill Clinton. It was an exhilarating experience!

My daughter, Courtney, who was ten at the time, became physically tired-- sleepy, irritated and bored. She could not believe that my husband and I were actually staying for all three services. She and her girlfriend, Cherae, who had spent the weekend with us, were ready to go home. However, I made it perfectly clear that under no circumstances were we leaving until we saw the President. Any other time, they would have gotten their way, but not this time. The playing could wait, the T.V. could wait, and the food could wait because we were about to embrace a piece of history just by being in the same room as Bill Clinton. And believe me, it was worth the wait! When he entered the sanctuary, there was a thunderous roar that permeated the building as the church received him with a standing ovation. Even the girls jumped to their feet, clapped their hands and grinned from ear to ear. It was a time to remember!

As usual, Bishop Thomas preached with much power. His sermon was titled, "The Gates of Hell Shall not Prevail Against Thee." Bishop preached so hard that it stirred everyone up, including President Clinton. When the President stepped up to the pulpit to give his remarks, I believe he stepped into the aftermath of the Holy Ghost and the anointing left by Bishop Thomas. On that day, the President experienced what it felt like to be standing on holy ground. Once he took hold of the microphone, he began to thank God for being in this anointed church, surrounded by spirit-filled people at one of the most critical points in his life. I believe he received and accepted this encouraging word as a prophetic announcement and declaration that despite all he had recently endured, he could be assured that God was still on his side and everything was going to be all right. One could literally see and feel the joy, excitement, and sense of renewed hope the President was experiencing. He seemed as if a heavy load had been lifted from his shoulders and he was now ready to take the reins and move forward to finishing his term as President. He took a text and began to expound on the word as if he was ready to preach the next sermon. He quoted scriptures and gave remarks like we had never heard him before. He brought the congregation to its feet; not because of some well-written, rehearsed, politically correct speech, but because he truly felt the presence of God. I am sure that his secret service men, staff advisors, and political colleagues had never seen that President Clinton before. He was truly grateful to be in God's house amongst His people.

When the service was over, we could still see security on foot, in cars, on the roof and in other strategic places. We saw the plane in which he arrived, securely hidden away in an open field behind the church. The plane was surrounded by armed security. The traffic was blocked, re-routed, and backed up for miles, but no one seemed to mind. Everyone was happy, patient, calm and extremely cooperative. It was truly an awesome time. I overheard one lady say, "I shook his hand, I actually shook his hand! I am never washing this hand again," as she laughed profusely with her family and friends.

While this truly was an awesome time and I really enjoyed recounting the experiences of that day, I did not randomly choose to talk about Bill Clinton in the first chapter of this book just for the sake of talking about him. I shared this story because I wanted to compare and contrast the willingness of our human nature to make sacrifices, spend money and be inconvenienced in order to come into the presence of man, but we sometimes find it too difficult, time consuming, and unprofitable to come into the presence of God.

I wanted us to think about the many weeks of planning and preparation that was needed in order for us to spend a couple hours in the same room as the president. And while I have carefully noted the visibly long lines, traffic jams, re-routed entrances into the church, the individual body and purse scanning procedures, planes, escorts, limousines, clothed and unclothed security, and the reserved seating of white house staff and officials, I am sure that I have only scratched the surface of all the extensive work and planning that occurred behind the scenes. I can only imagine the number of phone calls, e-mails, preliminary visits, and written correspondences that had to take place prior to this event taking place. A great amount of detail went into ensuring the safe arrival and departure of the President to and from New Psalmist Baptist Church.

As we begin to explore our human behavior more closely, I need for us to first put the president's visit into perspective. We know that Mr. Clinton is merely a man; a great man, a special man, but still a man of flesh and blood. Although he held the title and position as President of the United States, he was still a mortal man with imperfections. In fact, this was probably the worst time in his political career as he had recently been caught in a highly publicized adulterous relationship with Monica Lewinsky. This affair attracted media attention. It seemed like the media waged a personal attack on the President. Everywhere we turned, we found that this news was the talk of the day. The media consistently attacked and discredited his character, giving no regard to his position or his family. Most people were ready to move on and allow the President to get back to the business of handling the affairs of the country and to do what was necessary to try to make amends and preserve his family. However, there were some judgmental, non-forgiving individuals who thought that the President should be impeached, as they had decided that he was no longer fit for the presidency.

However, President Clinton had finally entered into a different kind of environment. He had come to the church. He was now in the presence of non-judgmental Christians who knew the power of prayer and forgiveness. He had come into the presence of individuals who welcomed him with love and forgiveness. We were able to receive him with forgiveness because we understood that we too served a God who lovingly forgave and continues to forgive us of our own weaknesses, indiscretions, and other sins. If we remain cognizant of our own need for forgiveness, then it is not too difficult for us to forgive others.

After reflecting on such a memorable day, my mind began to ponder on two pertinent questions: Why don't we prepare for the presence of God like we prepared for the President? Why aren't we excited about the opportunity and privilege to come into the presence of God like we were about coming into the presence of the President?

The irony of our human behavior deserves much introspection. We are aware that God is the creator of man. We understand that no creation is ever greater than its creator. So why is it that we, His creation, sometimes appear unaware as to how we should come into His presence? We are clear however, about the expectations for coming into the presence of men. Why is it that we seem to value our ability to be in the presence of certain people more than we value being in the presence of God?

We all know that man, no matter how great, could never do for us what God can. Yet, despite our knowledge of the omnipotence of God, we somehow still continue to have our priorities out of order. We sadly and unconsciously continue to give people and things precedence over our God. The purpose of this chapter is to give us something to think about. Oftentimes, we are moving swiftly throughout life without thinking about our actions. And when we do think about our misdirected actions, we quickly rest on our belief that God knows our hearts and God understands. Yes, God does understand. He understands that we make time for the things and people we love but not so much for Him.

While I do believe most of our behavior is unconscious, it is still inexcusable behavior. I believe that we are so caught up in our flesh--our wants and desires, that we really do not give much thought to our tendency to put God on the back burner. We have been reared in a culture that has caused us to be impatient and self-absorbed. We want what we want and we want it immediately. Prayer does not work that way. Although we may believe that God does answer prayer, we have no specific guarantee that our prayers will be answered the way we want it answered and we have no specified timeframe for which it will be answered. Thus, we fail to make the necessary sacrifices to spend time with God, read and study His word, and reverently come into His presence. We fail to do so because we fail to see the immediate benefits. We fail to totally trust God and know that He only does what is best for us, even if we do not understand it at the time.

Spiritual discipline is unlike the discipline we must have in other areas of our lives. For example, it is not too difficult for us to exercise discipline when we have to wake up early every morning to go to work. It is the guarantee that we will be compensated within a specific timeframe that forces us to go to work tired, exhausted, stressed, and even sick sometimes. It is the understanding that we will be compensated in a timely manner that causes us to drive long distances through rush hour traffic and give up forty hours of our life per week. We push ourselves because we know that pay day is coming. We push ourselves to get through the work week by praying to God, asking for healing, strength, energy, patience, wisdom, and whatever else we need to get through our week. However, I wonder how often we stop to take the time to thank Him for getting us through the week.

Spending time with God and preparing for His presence often requires time that we are unwilling to expend because we cannot pinpoint when we will be compensated or receive the benefits of our time spent with Him. God has not provided us with a yearly calendar that indicates the day our prayers will be answered, the day we will receive the promotion, the day we will marry our spouses, the day our loved ones will be saved, the day our circumstances will turn around, or the day our dreams will be realized. We do not know how long we must fast and pray, how long we must suffer, how long we must cry, how long we must wait, how long we must be alone, how long we must be passed over, or how long we must hold our peace. All we have to hold on to is the fact that God knows what's best for our lives—His timing is always best.

Spiritual discipline does not come with a specified timetable or instructions on how to obtain a specific thing at a certain time. Thus, we become impatient and move away from God because we do not see the immediate benefits. The fact is, God knows us better than we know ourselves. He knows exactly what we need, how we need it and how long we need to wait before we get what He has in store for us. God not only wants to bless us, but He wants to be sure that we are mature enough to handle the blessings when they come. Otherwise, we would wreck ourselves and those around us because we are not equipped to handle and sustain these blessings. If we want what God has for us, we must exercise discipline. Again, spiritual discipline is unlike discipline in other areas of our lives because it requires uncompromising faith, trust, patience, and tenacity. We must continue to persevere in faith even if we do not see the expected results.

I am grateful that God continues to be patient with us despite our impatience with Him. He stands by our side despite our inappropriate actions and misguided decisions to put others before Him. God continues to be faithful and merciful towards us. He amazingly and unassumingly comes into our presence without all the fanfare and the hoop-la. When God comes into our presence, we do not have to have our purses checked or our bodies scanned. We do not have to stand and wait for hours in long lines. God, unlike the President, does not have to be surrounded by security guards who must ensure that we do not get too close to Him. God does not need gunmen and helicopters on the roof. He does not send angels ahead of time to check out the environment to make sure it is safe. God does not have to enter the service through a certain door at a certain time. God does not have to sit in a specific seat with a certain person in the chair beside Him. God is not bothered or concerned with the logistical layout of the service. He just shows up.

The only thing that God needs to come into our presence is an invitation. What's even more amazing about God is that He does not only respond to invitations from just those individuals in leadership but from regular folks like you and me. One does not have to be the Bishop, pastor, preacher, teacher or deacon to receive a response from God. Those who invite Him into their presence do not have to sit in the pulpit with robes and collars or in designated sections on the floor with suits and hats. God is no respecter of person. He will come if you extend the invitation to Him.

God is not on any time restraints and He has no scheduling conflicts. He is always available. God will come wherever and whenever He is invited. He will come into our mess, our confusion, our brokenness, frustrations, struggles, and our helplessness. In fact, there is no situation too bad for God to enter in. Moreover, He will not only show up, but He will straighten things out. He does not come just to titillate us for a moment and then leave; He comes to make permanent changes that will cause us to lead more productive lives.

Now, I realize that I have over simplified these comparisons. It is not quite as simple as I have made it out to be. I realize that Bill Clinton is merely a man bound by the physical restraints of his own humanity. I realize that he held the highest office in the country, thus certain precautionary measures had to be taken to guard and protect his life. While on the other hand, I am talking about God Almighty, a spirit. There is no need to protect God from bodily harm. We know that God cannot be contained or restrained by anyone or anything. I have simply paralleled the preparations for the two visitors because I merely wanted to bring attention to the fact that we sometimes take God for granted. Too often we fail to give God the honor, reverence, and praise He is due. And I believe that it is high time for us to, once and for all, get our priorities in order.

We should always be cognizant of the need to honor and reverence the presence of our God. We should always be willing to enter the sanctuary with praise and thanksgiving. We should always be willing to saturate the atmosphere with true praise and worship. When we come into God's presence with a spirit of praise and worship, we make the atmosphere conducive for blessings. When we prepare the atmosphere for God's entrance, we better benefit from His presence because we have set the tone for receiving healing, deliverance and miracles. When we are able to fill the room with love songs for Him, physically bow down before Him, raise our voices and lift our hands towards Him, we will always be made better as a result of that worship and prayer experience. We must never take for granted our ability to come freely into the presence of God nor should we underestimate the value of God's willingness to come into our presence.

We should be ever so grateful that God will show up and commune with us wherever we are. We can openly communicate our feelings, thoughts, questions, and fears when we pray to Him. It is a wonderful gift that God has afforded us. It is quite phenomenal to comprehend the fact that we can live on earth and talk to God in heaven. When we spend time with God in prayer, it only makes us better. We cannot spend quality time with God (in prayer) and not feel an exhilarating high as a result of being in His presence. Nor can we spend quality time with God and not come away from that experience feeling more informed and refreshed. This spiritual encounter is the beginning of an on-going love relationship where the time sacrificed to spend with Him outweighs the benefits of any other activity or relationship in life. In fact, your relationship with God only enhances your relationships with others. Once you have an encounter with God, you are never the same. You are different, stronger, and better than you were before.

However, if we fail to spend quality time with God, we will never know His plans for our lives. And we will never develop a true relationship with Him. We must learn to pray and trust God to direct our paths. We must persevere in prayer by sitting still, waiting patiently, and meditating with a posture of anticipation and expectation. When we learn how to do these things consistently, it is amazing what God will do and how He will move in our lives.

When we pray more to God, He will begin to drop new ideas in our spirits and show us which direction to take. He will always lead and guide us into our destiny. We must strive to discipline ourselves to hear and obey the voice of God by continuously communing with Him through prayer.

Throughout this book, we will begin to explore other reasons why I believe that Christians fail to pray consistently and therefore are unable to hear God speak. I believe the more we talk to God, the more He talks back to us. The more we talk with God, the easier it is to recognize His voice. We must make it a priority to do whatever it takes to hear God clearly. It is crucial, in these times, that we are able to hear and recognize the voice of God. The Bible declares that His sheep know His voice. If you are His sheep you should know His voice. The self-examining question for today is…. Can I hear God? The next pertinent question is….Am I obeying God when He speaks?

# Chapter 1- Scriptures

1. Enter into his gates with thanksgiving, and into his courts with praise: be thankful unto him, and bless his name *Psalm 100:4 KJV*

2. But if you do not forgive others their sins, your Father will not forgive your sins. *Matthew 6:15 NIV*

3. But seek ye first the kingdom of God, and his righteousness; and all these things shall be added unto you. *Matthew 6:33 KJV*

4. What shall we then say to these things? If God be for us, who can be against us? *Romans 8:31 KJV*

5. And I say also unto thee, That thou art Peter, and upon this rock I will build my church; and the gates of hell shall not prevail against it. *Matthew 16:18 KJV*

# Chapter 2
## *Prayer – The Ultimate Gift*

# Chapter 2
## *Prayer – The Ultimate Gift*

Prayer is the ultimate gift because it is the only gift that can be given once, yet have the uncanny ability to give and keep giving over and over again; transcending both time and space. Not only does prayer transcends time and space, but it is so powerful that even death cannot prevent it from reaching its destination. Many of our forefathers prayed for freedom, change and deliverance for their people, but never lived to see the change take place. However, their prayers did not die with them but continued on in time and in space to reach the ears of God who heard and answered.

Our ancestors succumbed to slavery but refused to stop praying while enduring this ordeal. They not only prayed for strength to overcome their own plight, but they prayed and believed God for the day that their children's children would no longer have to suffer at the hands of slavery. Although many of them died, they never failed to lift up holy hands toward their God; walking by faith, trusting and believing that their collective prayers would reach heaven and bring forth victory for their people. They earnestly believed that one day God would remove the hand of slavery from the necks of their people. And although many of them never experienced freedom on this side of Jordan, we can thank God that their prayers did not die with them. Their prayers lived on, kept moving and traveling from generation to generation until the back of slavery was finally broken and all of God's people were free.

Prayer is an ultimate gift because we can give it to those we know and do not know. We have the ability to pray for people we have never seen and those whose names we do not know. We pray for an end to their hardships and struggles. We pray for their deliverance, we pray for brighter days and better living conditions for our brothers and sisters who reside millions and millions of miles away in distant and impoverished countries. If we do not have the finances to assist at any given time, we can always pray. We pray for positive leadership, democracy and educational opportunities for those who are oppressed. We pray for peace and religious freedoms for those who are surrounded by violence and dictatorship. We pray because we know that our prayers move; it reaches, it climbs, and it stretches across boundaries targeting specific situations and individuals who are in need of God's intervention. I am so grateful that prayer is not stagnant, but it travels across cities, states and countries, reaching those who God has laid on our hearts. If we love God, then we will love our fellowman. If we love our fellowman, we will lift them up in prayer. We will sympathize and empathize with their situations, consistently offering the gift of prayer to all who might feel alone, abandoned, overlooked and forgotten.

I am reminded of the lyrics of another song we sang when I was a child. The song said, "Somebody Prayed for me, had me on their Mind, they took the Time to Pray for me." The key word is somebody. Somebody took the time to pray. Somebody could be anybody who has a heart for God's people; who sees and understands that individuals and situations need the healing, saving hand of God. Somebody could be anybody who knows and understands the earthshaking power of prayer. When you are a prayer warrior, it matters not if you know the person, (their race, age, color or gender); you pray because there is a need. You pray because divine intervention is necessary and you need God to fix what you cannot. You pray because God has commanded that we pray one for another because at the end of the day, God loves us all. Our job is to pray and do it without ceasing; believing that God will do what we ask according to His will and purposes for our lives.

Prayer is the ultimate gift because it is precious, priceless and powerful. Prayer is in a class all by itself. It is so precious that it supersedes the value of diamonds, rubies, silver and gold. The value of prayer cannot be translated into carats or distinguished by letters and numbers that specify its clarity. Its value is beyond measure and never decreases over time. Not only is prayer precious, it is also priceless. Prayer cannot be measured in dollars and cents. It could never be bought, sold or auctioned off. This precious, priceless, powerful gift is so unique that it can only be given away or offered up. Prayer is so powerful that no man or written law can really prevent it from going forth. Laws might stop open public displays of prayer but laws cannot stop silent prayers. We can pray silently without uttering a sound. We can pray without anyone knowing that prayer is going forth. Prayer is its own entity unto itself; safely encapsulated in the spiritual auspices of God. Therefore, we do not have to have it insured or bonded because it will never be lost, stolen or misplaced. No one can take prayer away from us. Prayer is our communicative gift from God.

Prayer, although a precious gift requires no wrapping paper, flowers, balloons, bows, or cards, yet it is always beautifully packaged with the power and anointing of God. This gift can be delivered without postage and need not be handled by a mail carrier. It will never be delivered to the wrong address and it always reaches its destination on time.

This gift does not require technology. We need not have access to fax machines, scanners or computers to send or receive our prayers. Thus, the older generation need not fear being left behind due to their inability to keep up in a fast-paced, computer driven society. This gift still works wonders without all of the fancy gadgets. Prayer transcends technology. Therefore, it will never become outdated or be removed from the shelves because of technology upgrades. What's even more impressive about this ultimate gift is the fact that it is free. It is accessible to anyone who desires to have it and use it. The only thing that this gift requires is time and faith. We must be willing to take the time to pray for ourselves and others and we must believe in faith that our God will hear and answer the prayers that we offer up.

# Chapter 2 - Scriptures

1. Confess *your* faults one to another, and pray one for another, that ye may be healed. The effectual fervent prayer of a righteous man availeth much *James 5:16 KJV*

2. A new command I give you: Love one another. As I have loved you, so you must love one another. By this everyone will know that you are my disciples, if you love one another *John 13:34-35 NIV*

3. Pray without ceasing *1Thessalonians 5:17 KJV*

4. Now this is the confidence that we have in Him, that if we ask anything according to His will, He hears us. *1John 5:14 NIV*

5. Until now you have not asked for anything in my name. Ask and you will receive, and your joy will be complete. *John 16:24 NIV*

# Chapter 3
# *Seven Obstacles that Keep Us from Praying*

# Chapter 3
## *Seven Obstacles that Keep Us from Praying*

**Warning Disclosure:** Please pay close attention to the seven obstacles. Do not underestimate or disregard the subtle powers and abilities of these everyday obstacles that are designed to thwart and stunt our spiritual growth. Satan's plan is to obscurely prohibit us from praying and hearing God's voice. Satan does not want us to have that unshakable confidence and peace that come when we can hear and recognize the voice of God.

### Obstacle #1 – Distractions
Distraction – To draw one's thoughts or attention to something else; divert.

I believe that distractions are Satan's number one tactic aimed to keep Christians from praying. Oftentimes, we have the mindset to pray, study and meditate on God's word. We even have a desire to fast at times. We desire to integrate these spiritual tools into our daily lives because we understand that all of these things help to keep us connected to God and increase our spiritual strength. Most of us are sincere about our walk with God. However, we must understand that Satan, the prince of the air, is sincere about keeping us off track. He does not want us to realize our potential. He does not want us to know and experience the power we have in the Holy Ghost. He does not want us to open our mouths and begin to call things that are not as if they were. Satan will do whatever it takes to keep us from establishing a relationship with God. We must understand that God cares about us and everything that matters to us. God's role as father in our lives is significant. God is serious about loving, protecting, and providing for His children. He took the time to teach His disciples the Lord's Prayer, which always establishes relationship, first by beginning with "Our Father."

Have you ever witnessed a pastor or Bishop with a large congregation, who is surrounded by armor bearers and security guards, whose job is to keep others out, but somehow the pastor's children, no matter how small, are not concerned with these big strong men who guard the door? They realize that no one can deny them access to their father. Have you ever watched television shows where powerful men were conducting meetings with their top executives only to be interrupted by the secretary, who was given specific orders to not interrupt the meeting at any cost? However, the secretary rushed into the meeting with the phone in her hand to say, "Sir, it's your son/daughter who says that they must speak to you right away." Oftentimes, the father will stop the meeting and clear the room of all those important people, to address the concerns of his child. Satan does not want us to really understand that we are God's children and that He will clear the room for us. Therefore, Satan does whatever he can to keep us from praying and strengthening our relationship with God. He tries to cloud our minds so that we do not see how valuable we are to God. He will use anything or anyone to keep us off kilter and unfocused. For example, he will use our jobs, families, finances, health and even the church, to keep us from praying and doing what God has called us to do.

We can no longer be passive in our pursuit of God. We must be attuned and aware of the distracting tactics of the enemy. We must know that every time we decide to go on a fast, we will receive an invitation to dinner or the job will send us to a mandatory training, which will include lunch. We must know that an empty house, just right for prayer, will suddenly become invaded with family members who will enter the house yelling, "I am home!" We must know that once we shut and lock the door to pray, the phone will inevitably ring and although we know that there is a 95% chance that it is an unknown caller, our mind will convince us of the 5% chance that it is our child or a family member who may be in distress. When we stop praying to check the caller I.D., guess what? It was an unknown caller. We must realize that once we decide to read the bible, we will become bored and overcome with sleep. If we make up our minds that we will start getting up early for morning devotions, we should know that something will keep us up later than usual the night before. I could go on and on to list many more examples of the distractions we consistently face when we try to get closer to God, but hopefully you get the picture.

My aim is to keep these distractions at the forefront of our minds so that we will be cognizant of the devil's tactics. I want these distractions to stand out like red flags so that we can be prepared to guard against them, stay focused and keep praying. We must be diligent in pursuing the things that help us to become spiritually strong. In this way, we will be equipped to do and excel in all the things that God has called us to do and become.

**In Summary** – Do not be hindered by distractions; fight through them. Let the devil know that it will take more than a ringing phone, a dinner invitation, boredom or sleep to keep us out of the presence of God! We must let the devil know that we will persevere through all of his distractions.

### Obstacle # 2 - Time
Time- A system of measuring the passing of hours (standard time)

Where has the time gone? There is not enough time in the day. Time waits for no one. If only I had a little more time. How many times have we heard these statements? Better yet, how many times have we echoed these statements as we hasten to get the next thing done? I have come to realize that one of earth's most precious commodities is time. In fact, the older I get, the more precious time becomes. The world might refer to silver, gold, rubies and diamonds as earth's most precious commodities but I beg to differ. To have all of earth's precious gems without time to enjoy them is null and void.

God in His infinite wisdom has allotted us all the gift of time. It does not matter if we are rich, poor, Black, White, male or female; we all get the same number of hours per day. We all get 24 hours. It is up to us to maximize the time we have. Satan is an expert at getting us to believe that we do not have enough time to pray, to read, or to study the word of God. He makes us believe that we do not have time to go to bible studies and memorize scripture or invest in spiritual materials that will help us to grow in God. It is ironic how Satan will convince us that we do not have time to spend with God even though it is God who has given us the time in the first place. Let's just take a moment to ponder this thought. If we are too busy to spend time with the God who gave us the time in the first place, then surely we are just too busy. If we are too busy for God, then our priorities are out of order!

We must make a conscious decision to spend time with God. However, we must understand even after we have made this decision and have put forth our best efforts, we may still find it challenging to consistently follow through. Setting time aside can even be difficult for those who truly love the Lord. I am speaking from personal experience. I am a licensed Social Worker by profession and a Minister by calling. Both roles are geared towards helping, motivating, inspiring, encouraging, strengthening and empowering others. In order to be effective in these roles, one must have a genuine love and concern for people and their overall physical, emotional, psychological and spiritual well-being.

When you are a caring, selfless individual, it can be difficult to pull yourself away from the needs and demands of others. This constant desire to assist, encourage, support, teach, guide and direct can sometimes cause an individual to simultaneously be pulled in many directions and if not careful, one could fall prey to being used by others. Additionally, social workers and ministers have oftentimes been known to be strong leaders who possess good people skills and therefore are often sought out for their wisdom, advice, prayers, support and listening ear. They are also known for their knowledge, honesty, integrity, passion, confidence, and trustworthiness. Thus, they are constantly giving of themselves, which can often leave them feeling depleted. In the social work profession, we refer to this feeling as "Burn Out." We are taught to set limits, establish boundaries, and take time out for ourselves. Otherwise, we will be of no help to others. This phenomenon is the same in the spiritual arena. One must take time out to be spiritually refueled via prayer. Only God can sufficiently pour back into us what He has called us to give out.

Satan's tactic is to keep us so exhausted, from helping others and doing good, that we fail to take the necessary quality time with God for ourselves. Thus, we will become ineffective in our careers and in our ministries. Let me stop right here and clearly say that it does not matter that we know what we should do and can tell others how to do it if we fail to do it ourselves. Satan does not care that we are cognizant of our need to pull back from others so long as we remain caught up with doing good, to the point where we are too tired to pray and hear from God. We cannot be fooled by the time obstacle. We must find the necessary balance for our lives. Despite the challenge, we must learn how to say no and pull back from all of these competing external pressures and demands. I must admit that I personally struggle with this one, but I can hear what God is saying to me and all of His children. We must get this right. It is a subtle move for the enemy to get us so caught up in doing right until we are actually doing wrong. Think about it.

I believe that prayer is the answer. Prayer helps us to find that balance. After all, God made us and knows us-- our personalities and our makeups. Therefore, He can help us to know when to say "when." While I understand that to whom much is given, much is required, it is important that we realize that God is the giver so we must be intentional about getting what we need from Him first.

I have found that life can become overwhelming, depressing and stressful if we do not spend time with God. If we spend time with God, we will be strengthened to keep moving forward. When we spend the necessary time with God, He will help us to get the important things done and help us to let go of the things and people who are not as important as we once thought they were.

**In Summary** – If we are too busy to spend quality time with God because we do not have time in our 24-hour day to give a portion of that time back to Him, then clearly we are just too busy. We must check ourselves and re-evaluate our priorities. We must give God His time first and He will help us with the time we have left. Please keep in mind that God and God alone is the only one who really knows just how much time any of us have left.

**Obstacle # 3- Inconsistencies in our prayer experiences**
Inconsistencies – Not always acting or thinking in the same way; changeable

Sometimes Satan is subtle in his attempt to keep us from praying. He will use something as subtle as our different prayer experiences. For example, sometimes when we pray we can feel the presence and power of the Holy Spirit. Sometimes our connection with God is made quickly. We walk into our prayer rooms and it is as if God was just waiting for us to show up. Sometimes tears of repentance or tears of joy stream down our faces and we know or feel that our prayers have been heard and answered. We feel that our burdens have been lifted and we feel empowered to press on a little while longer. This type of prayer experience is rewarding. It is the type of prayer that will bring you back for more.

On the other hand, there are times when we pray and we do not feel anything. We stay in prayer a little longer. We change our physical positions by kneeling or standing. We pray silently and then we pray aloud, but we still feel nothing. Sometimes, we feel that we have just wasted precious time. We feel that our prayers did not go beyond the ceiling of our prayer rooms. In fact, it seems as if our prayers hit the ceiling and bounced back down to us. We wonder if God is listening or if He is even concerned about our affairs. This type of prayer experience can be discouraging because we took the time to come before Him but we could not feel His presence. We must not fall for this trick of the enemy. We must know that God sits high and he looks low. He sees us in our prayer closets and He is pleased that we have taken the time to commune with Him. He knows that there are a million other things we could be doing, but we made a choice to spend time with Him. We must know that His ears are inclined to the prayers of His children. His ears are not stopped up and He is not in need of any hearing devices. He hears our prayers and He will never allow our prayer time to be wasted time.

Another example of inconsistency in our prayer experiences is when we leave our prayer room confident that we have heard from God and we know that we have received the solution to our problems or concerns. There is nothing like leaving a prayer experience with our burdens completely lifted because we have received a direct answer from God or clear directions as to how to proceed in a matter. We are confident in our next steps because we have heard from God. Who or what do we have to fear when our marching orders have come directly from God? This kind of prayer is awesome! We always come out feeling special because the God of the universe has spoken to us. This kind of rewarding prayer makes it easy to spend time with God.

On the other hand, we sometimes leave our prayer experience just as confused and unclear of our next steps as we were before we started the prayer. Sometimes we know that we have heard from God, sometimes we think we have heard from God, and other times we are sure that we did not hear from God. All of these inconsistencies in prayer can affect our willingness and readiness to consistently spend time in prayer. We can overcome this subtle trick of Satan by remaining steadfast in our prayers. We must learn how to be patient and persevere in our time with God. We must stay there until His will becomes clear to us. Trust me, staying in prayer and waiting to receive a sure word from God will beat a guess or a maybe every time. As we familiarize ourselves with what the word of God says about prayer, we will be confident that God not only hears, but He answers our prayers. We learn that God truly cares about us and any time spent with God is good time that will always be beneficial to our sense of self and overall wellbeing.

The word of God helps us to understand that sometimes our prayers can be hindered or held up as a result of Satan being the prince of the air. As we learn about spiritual warfare, we learn that Satan will do whatever he can to keep our prayers suspended in the atmosphere. He cannot stop our prayers from getting to God but he can do things to delay them from getting to God. That is why we must be careful with whom we share our hopes, dreams and goals. Sometimes people will try to discourage us or attempt to put stumbling blocks in our way. And often times these intentional hindrances come from family members and those whom we call friends. However, when we become aware of Satan's tactics, we are better prepared to stay focused, trust God and endure in prayer despite our inconsistent prayer experiences, feelings and uncertainties.

**In Summary -** Do not try to put God in a box. There is no box big enough to hold Him. Do not try to predict what our prayer experiences should be like. Know that the word declares that God hears and answers our prayers. Our job is to pray until we get what we need from Him. We cannot rely on our feelings to dictate whether the prayer was effective. We have to trust the inerrant, infallible word of God that unequivocally states that God hears our prayers. That settles it. Who can rely on feelings anyway? We know that our feelings are unreliable, unpredictable, fickle and apt to get us into trouble if we allow them to rule. Trust God and His word. After all, it is God's word that will stand forever.

## Obstacle #4 – God remains silent
Silent – Not speaking or not talking much

Sometimes when we pray, God is silent. We pray, we wait, and we get nothing. There are times when we mistake His silence for not answering and we can become discouraged and delusional about what we think God's silence actually means. This silence or inability to hear from God can be troublesome and unnerving to individuals who are earnestly seeking God for answers and specific direction for their lives. This silence can be even more disturbing when an individual believes that an answer from God is needed within a specific time frame. This silence can also make us believe that we have done something wrong and therefore God is not listening or answering our prayers. Again, Satan will trick us into believing that God does not care. He will cause us to believe that God is aloof, unaware and unconcerned about the urgency of our needs or requests.

Over the years, as I have continued in prayer, it has become increasingly apparent that God's silence never means that He does not care. We must know and understand that God is always interested in our affairs. He is pleased when we seek Him for direction in determining how we should handle situations that occur in our lives. We should never believe that God is ignoring us or is merely uninterested. This is not the kind of God we serve. He is always interested in what we have to say. However, God is not governed by our time frames. Although we may believe we need the answer in a week, God is not stressed by our deadlines because He knows differently and He knows what's best for us.

Sometimes God's silence can also mean we already have the answer. In fact, God knows that He gave us the answer two weeks ago, but we have failed to slow down, be still, and meditate long enough to process or absorb what we heard. We are so busy asking and pleading that we have not taken the time to listen. Try being quiet sometimes. Oftentimes, the answers to our concerns are all around us. God always prepares us and gives us what we need before we realize we already have it. There is no need for God to give us answers or solutions to problems which are already in the inner recesses of our spirits and souls. We must learn how to tap into the Holy Spirit that lives within us. The spirit dwells in us to lead us and guide us in all matters of truth. The more acquainted we become with God, the better we will be able to trust the Holy Spirit that lives within us.

I liken this silence to a child asking his parent for the answer to a question that the parent is sure the child can figure out on his own. It is times like these when a parent might remain silent because the parent knows that his child can figure it out alone because the parent is aware of his child's strengths and capabilities. Sometimes God remains silent so that we can come up with the answer on our own. He knows what we are made of and He is confident that we will make the right decision. It is in these times that God requires us to draw from the spiritual knowledge and resources that reside within us.

A second reason I believe God is silent in our prayers is that He has given us free will. We ask God if we should choose option A or B, and we expect God to choose for us. God does not choose because he knows that we will be fine and we will be successful regardless of how we choose--A or B. God knows that we will do well with either choice because both choices are good. He also knows that we will do well because our motives are pure. The fact that we are asking God to help us to choose between two good things is indicative that we are on the right track and spiritually grounded because we are not making a choice about anything that is out of His will. Remember that all things work together for good to those who love God and are called according to His purpose. If we are earnest in our pursuit of God and the things of God, He will allow A or B to work out for our good. Trust Him, make a decision and move!

I am sure that there are probably a number of other reasons, not yet revealed to me, as to why God remains silent with our prayers. However, I believe the most crucial reason that God remains silent is because our prayer requests are too small. We are simply asking for less than what we need to get the job done or to accomplish our goals. Our minimal request might be a quick fix to a short-term concern, but clearly it is not the answer to the long-term problem or dilemma. We have become accustomed to asking for a slice of the pie when God wants us to have the whole pie. If God gives us one slice of the pie it will only serve our immediate need, but if He gives us the whole pie, it will serve our need for today and tomorrow and we will be able to meet the needs of someone else as well. In this instance, God remains silent because He wants us to understand who He is and what He is capable of doing for us. We must know unequivocally that God rewards all of His children who seek Him. Therefore, I believe that God remains silent to give us the time we need to make our proper requests known to Him. In other words, God remains silent until our myopic vision comes into spiritual alignment with the great vision and plan He has for our lives. God knows us and He knows when we are mature enough to handle more.

I equate this type of silence to a loving, wealthy and responsible father who has a conversation with his son away at college. The son takes the time to call his dad and asks the question, "If you do not mind, would you please put $100.00 in my bank account?" The first thought the father would probably have is, "What is wrong with this silly boy? Why would he call me and ask for only $100.00?" And to add insult to injury, say, "If you do not mind." I can imagine that the frustrated father would ignore the request and begin to talk to his son about his plans for the upcoming weeks. The father might ask his son about the places he planned to go, the books he needed to purchase, the upcoming campus events and the cost of the tickets etc., etc. After this discussion, I believe the father would then change the subject, ignoring his son's ridiculous request and begin to talk about the weather or update him on how the rest of the family is doing. After talking about a different subject, I can imagine the father saying okay son it was great talking to you, I look forward to talking to you again soon. At this point, the boy realizes that he did not ask for enough. I can imagine the son saying, "Hey dad what about the money and by the way can you make that $500.00 because he now realizes that $100.00 is not going to be enough. I can imagine that the loving father would say, "Sure son, I'll give it to you. I'll put it in the bank right away. And the next time, ask for what you need the first time." The father would say, "I love you son, I want the best for you. Do not ever question if I mind giving you what you need, it is a pleasure for me to give you what you need because I love you. Because I can trust you, I'll not only give you what you need but I will give you some of the things you want."

If an earthly father could love and care this much for his son, how much more does our heavenly father love and care for us?

**In Summary**- Do not get bent out of shape about God's silence. Let's not automatically assume that God is ignoring us because of some wrong we have done. Instead, think-- maybe, just maybe we have been doing something right and He just wants us to trust what we already know, Or, maybe He simply wants us to step back, re-evaluate the situation, realize who He is and what He is capable of and come back with a bigger request.

**Obstacle # 5 – God says "No"**
No – not so; I won't, I can't, I refuse, it isn't, etc.: opposite of yes

The word *NO* can be a difficult word to hear and accept. No one wants to hear the answer **no** when we are asking for something. We always want to receive a *yes* to our requests, no matter who we are making our requests to. Children want their parents to say yes, pastors want their leaders to say yes, leaders want their pastors to say yes, individuals applying for loans want banks to say yes, individuals interviewing for jobs want employers to say yes, individuals asking for a mate's hand in marriage want that mate to say yes, and so on and so forth. Everybody who truly wants something from someone is hoping and praying for a yes, but sometimes we get the dreaded *no!* No is the last word we want to hear. In fact, sometimes the answer *no* can be so devastating to us that even the thought that the answer could possibly be *no* could sometimes prevent us from asking for what we want. We would prefer to hear a *maybe, let me think about it,* or even a *not at this time but come back later;* anything other than a flat out *NO.* No is disturbing and disappointing to us, and if we let it, it could stop us in our tracks. We have to learn to accept the word *no* and move on-- let it go, or maybe try again at a later time. Whatever we decide to do with our *no,* we must not allow it to stop us. The word *no* is a powerful two letter word that we must not only learn to accept but we must learn to say if we are going to exercise the boundaries necessary to become and achieve all that God wants us to be.

Some people believe that God will never say *no* to us. I disagree. I believe that God will say *no* to us if we are asking for something that is contrary to His will for our lives. There are other times when we may be asking for something that might take us off His course. God wants to order our steps. Just as God opens doors for us that no man can shut, He can close doors that no man can open. However, I believe that these closed doors are always closed for our benefit even if we cannot understand it at the time. This is where your relationship with God, your trust in God and His word kicks in. We have to understand that if God says *no*, it is because He knows best. God's *no* is better than man's *yes* because God knows our future and He knows the plans that He has for us; which is never to harm us but to bless us. We have to learn to say *yes* and *amen* to God's *no*, no matter what we think or feel about the situation.

I am convinced that God says *no* when we ask for things that are contrary to His word, His statutes and His principles. For example, I do not care how fine he is, how compatible you think he is, how white his teeth are, how easily he makes you smile, or how he brightens up your day, if he is somebody else's husband you can forget it! God is going to say *no* to that prayer. God honors marriage and He will not go against Himself to give us what we want.

**In Summary**- God has the right to tell us ***no***. He is our father and we are His children. We must trust that our father knows best. God will tell us *no* when He has a better plan for our lives. God will also tell us *no* if we are asking for something that goes against His word, His statutes or principles. Do not be discouraged by God's *no's*; remain faithful and trust Him fully. More than likely, we will live long enough to thank God for the *no* we dreaded hearing and could not understand at the time we received it.

## Obstacle # 6 – We are too tired
Tired – Worn out; weary, a need for rest; exhaust

There are times when Satan will stop us from praying simply because we are tired. We are so tired that we do not feel like praying, period. We have had a rough day at the office, on the construction site, in the hospital, at the school, or wherever we have spent most of our day. Now we want to come home, put our feet up, drink a cold Pepsi, watch a good T.V show, catch up on the News, take a bubble bath or read a good book. We are legitimately tired and we feel that we deserve a little time to unwind. We believe that God is an understanding God. After all, He knows how rough and strenuous our day was. He also knows our hearts and He knows that we really want to pray, but we are just too tired to pray right now.

There is nothing wrong or sinful about being tired. We are human beings, made of flesh and blood, and we do get tired. However, we must be mindful of how often we put God off because we are tired. As I mentioned previously, I believe it can become easy for us to put God off because we do not see the immediate benefits of prayer and we cannot predict when our prayers will be answered. It is difficult for us to press our tired selves to do something if we are not sure how we will benefit from our pressing.

As tired as we may be, we still manage to go to the office, the construction site, the hospital, the school or the gym daily. How many times do we get up in the mornings, drag ourselves out of the bed, and whisper a quick prayer for God to give us the strength to do what we believe we have to do or want to do for that day? We push our way with God's strength and God's mercy to our various places of employment because we can predict our pay days. We push ourselves in the gym because we can predict a healthier/fit body, so we go tired. We do it despite our desires or need for rest. And we come home again and say God knows our hearts. Yes, He knows our hearts and He knows that we do what we want to do. We find a way to do what we think is important. We find a way to maintain contact with those who we love and care about. We call our loved ones when we do not feel like talking, and we visit them when we would rather be at home. It's all a matter of what we perceive to be a priority or a necessity. God is so good and so patient with us that He continues to wake us up each morning and strengthen us in our various pursuits, only to be put on the back burner time and time again. Let's get wise to this trick of the enemy. Let's press into our prayer time--tired, like we press to do everything else. Let us not forget that it is God who gives us the strength to do all the things that make us too tired to pray and commune with Him.

**In Summary-** We must be thankful that we serve a loving and patient God. However, we cannot continue to take Him for granted or take His kindness for weakness. God is God and He is in control of all that happens in our lives. We must make Him our priority. Give Him the time He is due. We should start our day with God in prayer, talk to Him in the middle of our day and end our day with God in prayer. Although we might not see the rewards of prayer immediately, we can trust and believe that good things are occurring in and around us as a result of the time we are spending with God in prayer. We should not allow tiredness to stop us from praying. We may be tired while praying but we end up feeling rejuvenated afterwards.

## Obstacle # 7 – We feel unworthy
Unworthy – not deserving; not fit or suitable

Sometimes Satan will cause us to believe that we are not worthy to come into God's presence. He will remind us of a sin we have committed, a lie we have told, a wrong act or deed, a lustful or evil thought and make us feel so bad that we are ashamed or embarrassed to ask God for anything. In fact, the devil will make us wonder how we could have the audacity to come into the presence of God with our requests after we have done what we have done. This is a major trick of the enemy because if he can make us feel unworthy to talk to our father, this is the first step to sabotaging our relationship with God. This is precisely why it is important and necessary to know what the word of God says about forgiveness. The word lets us know that God is always willing to forgive us of our sins if we sincerely repent of our wrong thoughts and deeds.

We must understand that we are saved because of the blood of Jesus Christ and it is His blood that puts us in right relationship with God. It is not about how good we think we are or how hard we work in the church. God already knows that we are not perfect. This is precisely why He sent His perfect son to die for our sins. We are not to willfully sin, we are not to make excuses for our sins, and we are not supposed to haphazardly ask for forgiveness knowing that we have no intention to stop doing what is wrong. But when we are genuinely sorry for our wrong doings, we must know that we are God's children and we can repent and come boldly to His throne for forgiveness.

We must also know that our mess-ups, slip-ups, and failures are no surprise to God. He knows what we are going to do before we do it and that is why He has already devised a plan for our escape. God has already devised a plan for us to get back to Him. God knows that we must die daily to sin and we must consistently strive to become more and more like Him; pressing towards the mark of the prize of the high calling in Christ Jesus.

Can you imagine what life would be like for our children if we disconnected ourselves from them every time they made a mistake or did something wrong? Can you imagine what life would be like for them if they said, "Mommy, I am sorry" or "Daddy, please forgive me" and we turned our backs on them? If we do not forgive our children, there will be no room for teaching moments, maturity or growth. As parents, we already know that our children will make mistakes, do some things that we are not pleased with, go to some places that we would not recommend, but we would never stop loving them or granting them forgiveness whenever they ask. If we love our children enough to work with them, hang in there with them, encourage them, pick them up when they fall, help them get back on track when they lose their way, then what do we think about our God? We cannot allow the devil to trick us into staying away from God because of a wrong we have done. We must repent and run back to Him. He will forgive us with open arms because we are worthy. Remember, He counted us worthy when we were yet sinners with no knowledge of Him. Because He deemed us worthy, He allowed His only begotten son to take on the sins of the world so that we might be saved.

**In Summary-** Be wise to the tricks that the devil uses to shame or embarrass us from coming into the presence of God. We must know our rightful place in God. We have to know that we are God's children and He loves us unconditionally. We have to know that God is willing to forgive our sins every time we ask Him. We must understand that the blood of Jesus has paid for it all. The devil has no say so about our relationship with God. We have the authority to put Satan under our feet, tell him to get behind us, and refuse to allow him to separate us from God. Although sin separates us from God, repentance brings us back!

Now that we have learned and reviewed some of the tricks and obstacles that Satan uses to keep us from praying, we will not be blindsided by him. Hopefully, we will quickly recognize these obstacles and be prepared to press pass them every time. We must fight pass these obstacles so that we will not be easily knocked off track. We must realize that Satan does not have the authority to keep us from praying to our father and our God.

In the next chapter, we will look at some additional benefits of prayer. While we may initially be praying to receive answers and direction about specific things, we will find that we will gain much more in the prayer process. When we learn to proceed in prayer, our spiritual growth and development are enhanced. The prayer process, in and of itself, causes us to become more faithful, stronger, and mature in our walk with God.

# Chapter 3 - Scriptures

1. But ye shall receive power, after that the Holy Ghost is come upon you: and ye shall be witnesses unto me both in Jerusalem, and in all Judaea, and in Samaria, and unto the uttermost part of the earth. *Acts 1:8 KJV*

2. For I know the plans I have for you," declares the Lord, "plans to prosper you and not to harm you, plans to give you hope and a future. *Jeremiah 29:11 NIV*

3. This, then, is how you should pray: "'Our Father in heaven, hallowed be your name *Matthew 6:9 NIV*

4. The grass withers and the flowers fall, but the word of our God endures forever. *Isaiah 40:8 NIV*

5. But when he, the Spirit of truth, comes, he will guide you into all the truth. He will not speak on his own; he will speak only what he hears, and he will tell you what is yet to come. *John 16:13 NIV*

# Chapter 4
# *Growing in the Process of Prayer*

# Chapter 4
## *Growing in the Process of Prayer*

### A Relationship with God Produces Growth

When we establish a rich and consistent prayer life, we automatically begin to grow and mature in God. We cannot consistently spend quality time with God and not be made better as a result. God is too awesome, too powerful and too loving a God to allow us into His presence without us positively benefiting from our time with Him. Our spiritual relationship with God is much like the physical or natural relationships we develop with our family members and friends. We cannot really get to know an individual without investing quality time with him or her. The more time we spend in the relationship the better we get to know the person.

When we spend quality time with an individual, we learn his/her personality. We learn what things make him/her happy or sad. We find out what makes that person tick and what things tick him/her off. When we spend quality time with a person, we will be able to determine if he/she is sincere, trustworthy and dependable or phony, untrustworthy and unreliable. We will be able to determine if they are intelligent, stable, and grounded or simple, unstable and flighty. Spending time with an individual helps us to determine what things we have in common and we also learn the things in which we differ. All of these things can be determined based on the time and energy put into the relationship. The more time spent in the presence of someone or communicating by phone, Skype, Facebook Twitter, or text, the better we get to know that person.

True bonafide relationships/friendships cannot be formed if one of the two individuals is not vested in putting in the time. Real relationships that are able to endure the test of time, I believe are founded on genuine love, trust and commitment. This kind of relationship is reciprocal. Both parties willingly give of themselves without keeping score. In fact, when one really cares about another individual, he/she looks for an opportunity to be a blessing to the other person. It gives the individual joy to see the other person smile and be happy, while it pains them to see the individual hurt or sad. Real love does not take advantage, use, abuse, or manipulate. And so it is with our relationship with God.

When we really establish a loving and committed relationship with God, it is not a one sided, superficial relationship where we only acknowledge Him if someone happens to ask us if we are saved or if we are a Christian. When we really love God, His name will come up regularly in our conversations because He is not considered to be a one-time act where years ago, we decided to give our lives to Him by confessing that He is Lord, but did nothing since that time to get to know Him better. When we really love God, we will not be ashamed of Him and we will not hesitate to give Him the credit, the praise and the honor for all of the wonderful things He has done in our lives. When we really love God and spend quality time with Him, a trusted and committed relationship is established. When we really love God, we will strive to do the things that are pleasing to Him and we will make every effort to refrain from the things that grieve His heart. A genuine love relationship with God is reciprocal. We will not only call on Him when we are in trouble, sick, lonely, or depressed but also when we are in good spirits and doing well. When we really love God, we will spend time with Him just because… Just because He is God: patient, awesome, caring, loving, honest, and true. He is anything and everything we will ever want or need Him to be. When we develop a cherished relationship with God, we come to know Him as father and friend.

When we truly love God, we will not try to use or manipulate Him into giving us the things we want. We will not see Him as a sugar daddy, an ATM machine, or a Santa Clause who only dispenses gifts. When we establish a relationship with God, we understand that He desires to spend quality time with us. He desires for us to get to know Him better through reading and studying His word and prayer. God wants us to really get to know Him so we are not easily fooled or discouraged by the adversary when things do not go as we plan. He wants us to be confident in who He is and in His word. He wants us to understand that no matter what, He loves us and He has our backs. In fact, He has all of us, every part of us, not just our backs. We can depend on God as He holds us safely in the palm of His hands. When we love God, we will enjoy being in His company just as we do those we love in the natural.

Once we have fallen in love with an individual, we will think about that person when he/she is not around. When we are not in that individual's presence, we will think about the good times we have shared and the wonderful conversations we have had. Because we enjoy being in their company, we look forward to spending more time with them and having deeper, more meaningful conversations. We begin to look forward to an exchange of thoughts, and perspectives. The more rewarding this relationship becomes, the more time we want to be in that individual's presence. This kind of bond or relationship is not easily broken. We will not allow anyone to casually come between us. And we will not sit by passively while others talk badly, degrade, or diminish our family member or friend. In fact, we will speak up for him, defend him and protect him at all costs because he is special to us. We can refute the negative talk and views of others because clearly they do not know our family member or friend like we do.

So it is with our relationship with God. When we really begin to spend quality time with God by communing with him daily, or every chance we get, a bond begins to form and we crave being in His presence; desiring to talk to Him and listening for Him to talk back to us. We will learn His characteristics and His ways—what pleases Him and what grieves His heart. We will not allow things or people to separate the two of us. We will love Him and cherish Him and we will not take Him for granted. We will think of Him and come into his presence in the good times as well as the bad. When we love God because of Who He is, we will honor and revere Him. This spiritual relationship fueled by love, honor, and respect, makes it difficult for us to willfully sin. When we truly love God, we try not to disappoint Him or disregard His statutes. And if by chance, we do fall short in pleasing Him, we will want to quickly apologize/repent and make things right with Him. He is merciful towards us and we know that His love for us is unconditional. When we really fall in love with God, we will want to study His word because His word is life and truth. The more familiar we become with God's word, the more familiar we become with

Him. Surely, this kind of relationship, undergirded by a rich prayer life, will not be easily broken!

## Additional Spiritual Tools Derived from Prayer

I believe there are some added benefits to having a strong, committed prayer life. When we learn how to make prayer a priority, how to persevere in prayer despite our physical or emotional feelings, when we remain focused and learn how to block out distractions, when we refuse to allow the devil to condemn us and keep us from coming into God's presence when we mess up, when we learn when to stop talking and just be still and wait patiently to hear the voice of God, there is a spiritual growth and development which occurs within us that causes us to be victorious. This kind of strong prayer life enables us to weather the storms of life without becoming unglued.

When we insist on praying, a solid foundation is established and a strong internal spiritual infrastructure becomes erected within us. Although the winds blow, the lightning flashes, rain, sleet and hail beat at our doors, we somehow remain steadfast and unmovable. We realize that these weather patterns will soon have to subside. There is something inside of us that lets us know that everything is going to be all right. We develop a "This too will pass" attitude. A strong prayer life allows us to dig our heels in and stay the course because we have come too far with God to turn around now. We might be shaken but we will not fall apart; we might shed some tears and endure some sleepless nights, but we will not give up. Although we might be misunderstood, falsely accused, and experience some hardships we did not deserve, we will not let go of God's unchanging hand. Intellectually, we may not be able to wrap our heads around the things we are experiencing, but we will not lose our minds, and even if we veer off course, we will not stay off course for too long because our internal (spiritual) navigation system will always bring us back to the path that God has set before us. We always fall back in line because somehow we understand that our steps really are ordered by God.

When we remain diligent in prayer, there is something inside of us that reminds us that we are victorious and nothing can stop us as long as we hold on to Jesus. In fact, turbulent times cause us to hold on tighter and dig in deeper. This is when we put our game faces on, clothe ourselves in our spiritual armors and prepare for the fight. And although we might get hit hard enough to literally be knocked to the ground, we somehow know that we are going to get back up again. This kind of spiritual growth and security is what the elder members of the church referred to as, "A Know So Salvation." They knew they were saved and they had a strong conviction about the God in whom they believed. They had made up minds to go all the way with God. When they stepped into the ring they had every intention of going the distance. They knew that the tenth round would find them standing victoriously with their hands lifted high because they knew they were on the winning side. We need to understand that we too can believe God like the saints of old because we serve the same God. And although we might be fighting some twenty first century devils, they too must fall!

There are many added benefits or spiritual tools we gain in the process of prayer. In the prayer process, we not only get the things that we petition God for but we learn how to grow and mature in God. When we begin to pray consistently, we learn how to genuinely trust God, we learn how to wait, thus our patience is developed, we gain an increase in our faith, our self-confidence is enhanced, and we gain an overall sense of peace. When we persevere in prayer, we gain more than what we were looking for. There are at least five spiritual tools we gain that are beneficial for our success, growth and development on our spiritual journey. The five spiritual tools we will talk further about are: faith, trust, patience, self-confidence and peace.

**Faith** - 1.Confident belief in the truth, value or trustworthiness of a person, idea, or thing. 2. Belief not based on logical proof or material evidence.

When we pray, our faith is increased. The very fact that we are willing to speak openly or privately to a God that we cannot physically see or touch is a very basic but powerful indication that we have faith. Prayer substantiates our belief in God. When we pray to our God, we have to believe that He is all-powerful, all knowing, and everywhere at the same time. We must believe that He is omnipotent, omniscient, and omnipresent because we realize that while we are praying for one thing, countless others are praying for multiple other things too. However, our faith allows us to believe that He hears us all simultaneously while addressing all of us individually, without getting any of us confused.

Our faith causes us to believe that He is genuinely concerned about us and He is willing and able to grant us our requests. We are confident that God can hear, handle, and respond to everyone's prayer requests while still maintaining His daily activities of running the world. He causes the sun to rise in the mornings and set at dawn. He decides when to send the rain, hail, snow, or sleet. He commands the winds to blow, flowers to bud, and trees to grow. He does all of these things, while still ensuring that the sparrows are fed. We believe that our prayers are not interrupting God's bigger plans for who He allows to be born into the earth and those He allows to be taken out of the earth. Our faith in God causes us to believe that God is capable of doing all of these things without becoming overwhelmed or burdened like us. Therefore, we have learned how to take our burdens to the Lord in prayer and leave them with Him.

Most of us have come to the realization that we were not built to handle the pressures of life alone. We have learned that our attempts to consistently handle things, correct things, or make things happen often have a way of showing up in our bodies in the form of headaches, heart palpitations, heart attacks, high blood pressure, cancers, under-eating, over-eating, weight loss, weight gain, diabetes, high cholesterol, memory loss, pacing floors, sleepless nights, agitation, frustration, isolation and depression, just to name a few. Our experiences have taught us to pray. We do not pray one time and stop, but we pray all the time. I believe the more consistent we are in our prayer lives; the more our faith is increased. It is increased because we have witnessed and experienced our prayers being answered. We benefit from our prayer time with God even if we cannot articulate the immediate gains. Prayer time is always productive time because time spent with God is never wasted time.

However, there are some rewarding prayer experiences that significantly cause our faith to increase. These are times when we know without a shadow of a doubt that we have been changed. These are the times when we come to the prayer experience feeling one way but we literally leave feeling another. When we personally and tangibly leave our prayer experience feeling better and stronger, our faith automatically increases. Our faith increases because we can directly attribute these positive feelings to God and prayer. Every time we come to God with our petitions and He grants them to us, our faith is increased. Every time God answers one prayer, it inspires and encourages us to continue to pray and believe Him for more answered prayers.

When we go to God in prayer, we should not be asking God to do things we are capable of doing ourselves. If God has equipped us with knowledge, strength, talent, and wisdom to get the job done, then He expects us to do it. Too often, we sit back and wait for God to do what God is waiting for us to do. For example, if we want a job we should be filling out applications and submitting resumes. Then we can pray for God to open the door of opportunity to the prospective places of employment. If we want to buy a house, we should be saving money, establishing a good credit score, paying off unnecessary debt and determining where we want to live. Once our finances are in order and we have made a bid on the house, then we can pray for favor that our bid will be accepted.

When we pray we should be praying for God to open doors, make ways, and fix problems that we are not capable of handling ourselves. Our faith truly increases when we are faced with a problem we know we cannot handle and there is no one we can call to fix the problem for us. These situations are ideal for increasing our faith because we know that we lack the capability and the resources to get the job done ourselves. In situations like these, we understand that the problem will not and cannot be resolved without God's divine intervention. When this kind of prayer is answered, we know and acknowledge that nobody but God could have done this for us. During these times, we give God all of the praise and the glory and our faith grows in leaps and bounds.

I believe that our faith will continue to increase in the prayer process even if every prayer is not answered to our satisfaction. This happens because when we look back over our journals of prayer requests, we will find that more prayers were answered to our satisfaction than those that were not. We will also find that although some of our prayers were not answered the way we wanted or anticipated, it did not matter because somehow everything still worked out for our good. Oftentimes, we will find ourselves thanking God for not answering our prayers or opening the door to the thing we thought we wanted or needed at the time.

Faith also comes by hearing the word of God. It also comes from hearing the testimonials of others who share the results of answered prayers and miracles that God has performed in their lives. When we hear the man or woman of God, preach the word of God with truth, power and conviction our faith increases. When we hear other Christians tell of the mighty works they have witnessed God perform in their lives, our faith is increased. Our faith increases because we understand that God's word is true.

Most importantly, faith is increased when we hear God speak to us in prayer. Our faith is magnified when God speaks specifically to us about our particular situation. When God gives us the answer, the direction, the strategic plan or solution we so desperately longed for, our faith grows. God has a way of speaking a word, a phrase, or a directive that instantly changes our situations. The situation is immediately changed even if we cannot see the physical or natural change in our environment yet. We know that change has occurred when we see change within ourselves. We are no longer the same. We feel differently about the situation or issue, we gain an entirely different perspective or outlook about the situation that we could not see while we were worrying and trying to figure things out on our own.

God has a way of shedding light on dark situations and giving us peace about things that have been troubling us for years. Only God can orchestrate the perfect plan within a matter of seconds. And His plan always brings about the desired outcomes. His plan will always blow our minds because it is fail proof. When God gives us a plan, we can hardly wait to implement it because we are excited about the outcome. We are privy to results that no one else has knowledge of--Talk about having an inside scoop! We have not had the inside scoop until we have gotten it from God. It is this kind of prayer experience that confirms God's word that His ways are so far from our ways. We could not have come up with His plan or solution in a million years.

Our intellect is no comparison to the knowledge and the wisdom of God. He has a way of making those enormous problems and concerns that were so stressful and overwhelming to us at one time, seem so small and insignificant. When we hear God speak to us in our prayer experiences, it is like getting a triple boost of faith. The truth of the matter is, God's voice is powerful, and life changing. When God speaks to us, we are different because we know undoubtedly that God has spoken. When God speaks, it settles everything. Yes, everything is really settled. I cannot say it any simpler. The voice of God brings calm, peace, wisdom, enlightenment and revelation that significantly increase our faith.

**Trust** – A strong belief that some person or thing is honest or can be depended on: faith.

When we pray, our trust in God is heightened. Trust and faith work together. They are closely related as indicated in our trust definition. It is impossible to have faith in a thing or person and not trust it or him. Likewise, it is impossible to trust in a thing or person that you have no faith in. The more we pray, the more we trust God. We trust God more and more because He continues to prove Himself to be honest, dependable, faithful, reliable, and trustworthy. Our prayer experiences teach us firsthand that God is true to His word. We learn that we can trust Him to stand by every word written in the Holy Bible.

Life sometimes has a way of weighing us down. There are times when we feel that the pressures of life are too heavy for us to bear. Sometimes we feel that no matter how hard we try, no matter what efforts we make, changes we try to implement, or how much positive self-talk we use, life, family, friendships, church, and jobs continue to put more demands and expectations on us, causing us to feel like we are always trying to play catch up. Sometimes it becomes extremely difficult to find any time to meet our own spiritual, physical, social, psychological and emotional needs. Thus, the poignant question becomes, "When am I supposed to find the time to focus on my own needs, my own goals, my own health, growth and development?" The effort to balance life and its demands can be most challenging. I liken it to the hamster on the spinning wheel which runs faster and faster but somehow still remains in a place where little to no progress is made. It is in these times that we must trust God. We must go to God in prayer and ask Him for His help.

In the prayer process, we begin to ask God for strength, understanding, patience, wisdom, peace, boldness, and direction. We learn to trust God when we receive strength for a journey or a task that we knew we lacked the energy, will, or stamina to complete. We learn to trust God when we witness Him giving us understanding and clarity about individuals, statements or situations which left us confused. We learn to trust God when we watch ourselves go through experiences, trials and tribulations that cause us to grow in patience and wisdom. We learn to trust God when we see ourselves stepping up and speaking out with confidence and boldness in situations where we were known to have taken a back seat or faded into the background without taking any position or stance. We learn to trust God when we pray for direction and we witness God guiding us; clearly pointing us to the people or places He desires for us to be. The more we pray, the more we see ourselves growing in these areas. It is these answered prayers that help us to trust God more.

No one knows us like we know ourselves. We know our strengths, weaknesses, and insecurities. We know the areas in which we are comfortable and the people with whom we flow best with. We know when we are real or just faking it. We know when we are accepted or just tolerated. We know when people care or are just going through the motions. Because we know who we are and where we fall short, we ask God to build us up where we are weak. We ask God to help us build character, integrity and self–esteem. And when God answers our personal prayer requests of self-development, when we witness the change in ourselves, we know that we are praying to a God in whom we can trust and depend. We see His work first hand in us. It is one thing to see a change in others but it's a whole different thing to see the change in ourselves.

Have you ever heard someone say, "I remember the day when I would have told that person where to go and how to get there?" Have you heard someone say, "The old me would have done this or that?" Have you witnessed someone say, "I know that I have been changed because I would not have taken this or that off of her?" More importantly, have you said similar statements yourself? Therefore, you know you are saved because you know you have been changed. And we know that no one could have brought about these changes in us but God.

The more we study God's word, the more we learn of His ways and attributes. We know that God is a God who cannot lie. He moves in miraculous ways: He opens doors that we knew were shut; heal those who are sick, and bring about justice for those who were done wrong. It is when we witness circumstances and situations being turned around that the trust factor increases in God. All of these things help us to know that we serve an honest God. A God that is true to His word. Prayer teaches us to take Him and His word literally and in doing so, our trust in God becomes unshakeable. We understand that if we can trust no one else, we can trust and depend on God. We can trust God because He is honest and dependable. He is Faithful to His word and He is faithful to His people.

**Patience** - The ability to bear pain, trouble, waiting, boredom, etc. and at the same time keeps calm and not complain.

When we pray, our patience is developed. The prayer process teaches us to be patient. We learn what it means to wait because often times our prayers are not answered as swiftly as we would like. Usually when we pray about a person, thing, or situation, we really are looking for immediate results. We want God do what we know He is capable of doing and fix the person, the thing, or the problem right away. We want God to do what the bible says He is willing to do. Most times, we have already conjured up in our minds the way we believe the problem should be resolved. And now we are just waiting for God to carry out our plans. When we finally decide to turn things over to God, we want and expect God to quickly grant us our petitions.

However, the prayer process teaches us that our timing is not God's timing and therefore, we must bear the trouble, problem, or concern until God answers our prayers.

Although the act of waiting can be difficult in and of itself, the ability to wait calmly without complaining is even more difficult. It is difficult to wait because we have been dealing with the problem or situation on our own prior to making the decision to take it to God in prayer. Maybe we have tried to talk to and reason with individuals. Maybe we have even worked tirelessly for weeks, months, and even years to resolve a problem or come up with an amicable solution. We may have also solicited direction and advice from others to no avail. Once we have exhausted all of our options and we conclude that this problem or issue is too big for us to handle, then we decide to take our concerns to God.

Now that we have finally come to Him, we want Him to intervene on our behalf and resolve the situation immediately. What we fail to realize is that God needs time to correct and undo some of the mess we have made in our efforts to fix things on our own. After all, it is not God's fault we waited so long to come to Him. He was there all the time waiting for us to seek Him for help. While God is pleased that we have decided to come to Him, He is God and He will fix the problem His way and in His time.

While our patience is being developed, over time we will come to realize that some prayers will be answered quickly, while others will take a while. Our prayer experience will sometimes give us the joy of having our prayers answered immediately. We will find that God sometimes gives us the answer to our problems while we are yet in the midst of the prayer. Other times, we will find that our prayers are answered shortly after we have prayed. There will be times when we get up from our prayer experience, we will find that while we were praying God was working things out, changing minds, and moving things around. There are other times, however, when we will find that we will pray repeatedly and it will seem as though God does not hear us because we do not have the solution or see the outcome of our prayers.

When we are faced with these scenarios, we will not become discouraged because we have a prayer history with God. We have seen God come through for us time and time again. We have witnessed the changing of people and situations. We have prayed long enough to know that He may not come exactly when we want Him, but whenever He gets to us, it will be right on time. The prayer process has taught us that answered prayer will always be on time because His time is always the right time.

**Self-confidence** – Sure of oneself; confident of one's own ability

I am convinced that we cannot spend quality time in the presence of an almighty, all-powerful, all knowing God and not receive a boost in our own confidence. Once we really understand who God is, He has a way of helping us to understand who we are as well. After all, we are His children and we are made in His likeness.

Individuals who are rich, powerful, and prestigious have a way of influencing the confidence of their children. These children are exposed to the best things that life has to offer. They wear the most expensive clothing, dine at the finest restaurants, meet and mingle with other influential and prestigious individuals. This exposure to greatness influences the children's thought processes, broadens their horizons, and inevitably boosts their self-esteem. You cannot grow up around greatness and not be affected by it.

In the natural, parents have a great impact and influence on their children. This influence might be positive or negative. It might be direct or indirect, intentional or unintentional. Whatever the case might be, parents significantly shape and influence the lives of their children. We become the individuals we are as a result of our genetics and our environment. Because of our biological make up or DNA's, we have some innate skills, abilities and talents. There are some things we can do and achieve easily without struggle just because we have been genetically wired to excel in that area. Our genetics can influence our wills and our dispositions. Our genetic make up is precisely what makes us who we are and not someone else. It separates us from some and makes us uniquely different from others.

We are also who we are as a result of our environments. There are some behaviors we have learned because we were exposed to certain situations and circumstances. The outcomes of these experiences have a way of shaping our thinking, our goals and ambitions, and our beliefs about ourselves. Not only do these experiences shape our perceptions of ourselves, but they shape our beliefs about our world. Two individuals could experience the exact same thing at the exact same time, but be affected differently because of their unique make up and their perception of their environments. How many times have you wondered how siblings reared in the same household, with the same biological parents, turn out to be so different? These siblings were reared with the same morals, values, guidelines and expectations; they saw the same things, heard the same messages, lived in the same neighborhood, played with the same friends, attended the same schools and yet they are so different. One child might turn out to be a caring, responsible, empathetic and reliable adult, while the other might turn out to be non-caring, irresponsible, unreliable, cold, aloof and angry.

This difference occurs because while the environment might have been the same and the parents were the same, each child's evaluation, perception or reaction to those experiences was different. Additionally, each child may have been more or less influenced by the negative or positive characteristics and attributes of either parent. Sometimes a child makes a conscious or unconscious decision to be more like one parent rather than the other or he might choose to take a little of something from both. Whatever the case might be, we might easily see a sibling group that behaves unbelievably different from one another. Ultimately, these individual choices and experiences will directly or indirectly affect and impact the individual's successes and overall sense of confidence.

And so it is with God. If we understand that we are His children; that He loves, protects, and cares for us; that He only wants the best for us (physically, spiritually, and emotionally) we would then be able to comprehend the insurmountable benefits of His influence. The major difference between God's influence and our parents' influence is that God's influence is only positive. God has no negative dispositions, behavior or characteristics. We can only receive good influences from God because that is all that He has to offer. In fact, if we gravitate towards Him and make an effort to be like Him, we automatically begin to think more of ourselves. We cannot be more like Him and love ourselves less. We cannot be in His presence and feel less than; we cannot take on His attributes and not be confident. In fact, being in God's presence will not only make us more self-confident, but it will help us to supersede the negative influences of our immediate environments. In other words, we might be surrounded by negativity but we won't be affected by it.

When we have reached a certain level of spiritual maturity, we know who we are and we understand, to some degree, what we are capable of achieving. I say to some degree because God is always stretching us and showing us that there is so much more to us than we could ever imagine. When we depend on God, He takes us higher by expanding our territories and influences. He helps us to believe that the impossible is actually possible. God's influence makes us secure and confident because we have been communing with Him. There is no one greater to commune with. There is no one more powerful, influential or knowledgeable than our God. He alone will unconditionally have our backs through the ups and the downs of life.

We always benefit as a result of a consistent prayer life. Over the years, I have heard some great motivational speakers. Speakers who will have you charged up, excited, inspired and ready to immediately achieve your goals and dreams. However, that charge and enthusiasm quickly dissipates after the speech is over. In fact, in many instances, the motivational speaker has not made it to the bank to cash his/her check before you are no longer motivated to achieve that goal or dream. This is not to speak negatively about motivational speakers; I believe they have their place. However, it is difficult to stay motivated because there are so many competing thoughts, ideas, problems, assignments, and situations that demand our time and attentions. Thus, it is easy to leave one room charged up and ready to go, but get to the next room with little energy, motivation or stamina to do anything. In fact, we will find at times that we have forgotten half of the things we have heard.

However, when we have heard a word from God, it is different from any preacher or motivational speaker. When we have heard directly from God, we will be inclined to treasure that word and rehearse it in our minds and in our spirits. We will remember the word verbatim, and every time we think about it, it becomes more real, more tangible and more achievable because it came from God. We know that we have an effective word with definitive positive outcomes and solutions. We know emphatically that this is a good word and a workable word because it came from God; God, who knows all things and does all things well. We must understand the importance of holding on to what we have heard. Satan will try to steal this word by distracting us to the point where we forget what we heard God say. As I mentioned previously, Satan will strategically use people, things, and situations to keep us off course. The adversary understands that it only takes one word from God to make a difference in our lives and situations.

Can you imagine what this world would be like if all Christians effectively communed with God, heard His voice and followed His directives? Just one word from God can totally change the trajectory and direction for our lives and the lives of those that follow for generations to come. Every time we pray, hear and obey God, we reap the benefits in every aspect of our lives. These positive outcomes and assurances ultimately help to build our self-worth.

**Peace** – calm or quiet.

When we spend time in prayer, we begin to have a life that embraces a peace that surpasses our understanding. In other words, a strong committed prayer life helps us to keep our calm, stay positive and remain hopeful in situations that would typically get other people roused up. A strong committed prayer life helps us to stay focused on achieving positive outcomes despite the difficulties we encounter in life.

Prayer helps us to remain in peace because we are able to focus on the prize and not the problem. Prayer helps us to realize that big problems come to hinder and prevent us from obtaining our dreams and aspirations. Because we are aware of the enemy's tactics, we become even more intentional about achieving our goals. We see obstacles as they are and we figure out a way to fight harder and remain focused. We are not easily dissuaded because we do not have a quitting mentality. In fact, obstacles cause us to fight harder and inspire us to become more determined. Our prayer experiences help us to foster a sense of inner peace because we are able to somehow get a glimpse into our futures. We perceive that things will get better and, circumstances will change, if we would just stay the course.

Prayer helps us to develop a win- win mentality because we know that if we are with God, then we are already on the winning side. It is a win-win situation because no matter how a situation starts out, we know that it always ends up working for our good because we love the Lord. We are assured that everything will work out, even if it does not look good or feel good right now. Our trust and faith in God helps us to remain steady. We are always looking for God to strengthen us, build us, and vindicate us in every area of our lives. Prayer helps us to literally believe in our heart of hearts that God truly has not brought us this far on our journey to leave or abandon us now. Thus, we are able to anticipate victory over every situation. Our experiences have taught us that we can depend and trust our God.

The peace of God supersedes what is happening in our immediate space. This is because we have learned to put our faith, trust and confidence in the God that we know. We know Him because we have developed a solid relationship with Him. We greet Him in the morning and we talk to Him throughout the day. We wait to hear Him speak back to us, guide and direct our paths. We are obedient to His word and His promptings, which causes us to be direct recipients of His grace, mercy and blessings. We have learned to say good night by thanking Him for His love, strength, kindness and direction throughout our day. We realize that we have accomplished all that was accomplished because of Him.

When we have this kind of relationship with God, we do not have to worry about unsupportive, non-nurturing, parents, spouses, friends or leaders. We know that men have their picks and they decide who they will help, mentor and support. The fact that they have not chosen us is oftentimes no reflection on us, but could be a reflection of that individual's own insecurity or need. Sometimes people pick those whom they can manipulate or control and those whom they expect to receive something in return. But the good news is that we serve a God who is not a respecter of persons. He loves us all and gives us all a fair shot. God has no insecurities or hidden agendas. God's only requirement is that we seek Him. If we seek Him, He will be found and He will give us the desires of our hearts.

When we realize that God really is in charge, then we can take hold of the fact that He really does have the final say over every situation. It is not those who occupy powerful positions who determine our fate or destiny; it is God. Therefore, our prayer lives force us to turn our anxieties, frustrations and disappointments over to God and He always works things out for our good. Knowing that we have God on our side is more powerful, energizing, and satisfying then trying to gain the affections of men. Our understanding of God's genuine love, affection and concern will always bring us incomprehensible peace.

Peace is a most sought after commodity. However, it is not often found or maintained without God. There are many things that people do, or buy to obtain peace. However, this kind of peace is temporary and only lasts for a moment. Money, people, power and material possessions can bring us peace for a short time, but God can give us everlasting peace when we stay in constant prayer with Him. His peace can be sustained throughout the test of time. Without peace, our lives are chaotic, stressful and full of worry, doubt and fears. Without peace, we stay off balance because we try to fix and make sense of things that we should be giving to God. Prayer helps us to release what we cannot handle.

I am not saying that if we pray our lives will be perfect and void of problems. But what I am saying is that prayer sparks something deep down on the inside of us that lets us know that somehow everything will be alright. We have an underlying notion that somehow we are going to be okay. We know that God is a present help and He will never leave us alone. There will be times when we might feel alone but prayer and knowledge of God's word helps us to know that we cannot rely on our feelings but we rely on the truth of His word. Because we have come to know what we know about God, based on our relationships, experiences and understanding of His word, we are able to get to a state of peace much quicker. We realize that there are some things that we cannot fix and some burdens that we cannot carry; however, we have learned that we can put those things in God's hand and leave them there.

I chose to write about peace last in the prayer process because I believe that we will only reach this level of peace and homeostasis once we have mastered the other tools first. It is after we have remained persistent in our prayer life and have developed unshakable faith, unquestionable trust, relentless patience and an unmistakable confidence in God and ourselves that we finally obtain an overall sense of peace. The more we pray, the more these things become etched in our spirits and in our lives. It becomes a part of us, who we are, and what we believe. We are living proof that prayer works because of our individual and collective experiences with God.

## Chapter 4- Scriptures

1. Consequently, faith comes from hearing the message, and the message is heard through the word about Christ. *Romans 10:17 NIV*

2. And without faith it is impossible to please God, because anyone who comes to him must believe that he exists and that he rewards those who earnestly seek him. *Hebrews 11:6 NIV*

3. Trust in the LORD with all your heart and lean not on your own understanding *Proverbs 3:5 NIV*

4. Study to show thyself approved unto God, a workman that needeth not to be ashamed, rightly dividing the word of truth. *2 Timothy 2:15 KJV*

5. And the peace of God, which passeth all understanding, shall keep your hearts and minds through Christ Jesus. *Philippians 4:7 KJV*

# Chapter 5
## *How Does God Speak Today?*

# Chapter 5
## *How Does God Speak Today?*

### The Bible

The Bible is the primary way that God speaks to us today. The Bible is the oldest, most read, revised, multi-translated, bestselling book that exists today. It is the sacred book of Christianity. It was written many, many years ago, but it is still relevant and applicable to life and all of its challenges in the 21st century. The Bible is the word of God. It is inerrant, infallible, and God breathed. It consists of the Old Testament and the New Testament. There are a total of 66 books in the Bible; thirty-nine books in the Old Testament and twenty-seven books in the New Testament. The bible is broken down into five sections: the Torah or Pentateuch, the Major Prophets, the Minor Prophets, the Psalms and the Poets.

Only a God-inspired book could remain on the bestseller's list throughout the ages of time and still remain relevant and applicable today. God being the omniscient

God, inspired man to write the 66 books of the Bible, over two-thousand years ago. This book continues to direct and influence our lives today. The Bible declares that everything on earth will pass away but God's word will stand forever!

If we want to know what God is saying, we must read the Bible. The written word of God is known as the Logos word. The word of God clearly teaches us how we should live our lives, love, and treat each other. The Bible provides us with examples of how Jesus lived while He was on earth. It shows how Jesus demonstrated love towards His fellowman by teaching, guiding, healing, blessing, and protecting them. The Bible demonstrates the unconditional love and compassion that God has for His people. We are to use Jesus as our example for how we should live our lives today.

The Bible is also filled with real life stories of men who desired to follow God but had shortcomings. We can read about men who struggled with their flesh just as we do today. They struggled with anger, jealousy, covetousness, greed, disobedience, immorality, doubt, promiscuity, fear and pride. Just because these men struggled in their flesh and often fell short of the glory of God, it did not mean that they did not love or want to please God. Scripture lets us know that often times when we desire to do good, evil is always present. Thus, we understand through God's word that there is always a constant struggle or war between the spirit and the flesh. God loves us despite our failures, insecurities and setbacks. However, He wants us to learn how to bring our flesh under subjection to His spirit. The Bible teaches us ways to discipline ourselves so that the spirit will rule more than the flesh.

God knew that we could not be victorious against sin on our own and allowed His only son, Jesus, to die for our sins. If we accept Jesus Christ as our personal Savior then we will be saved. The bible also teaches us about the power of the Holy Spirit which helps us to walk upright and trust God. This ultimately leads to victorious living in Christ Jesus. The Holy Spirit, also known as the Comforter, leads and teaches us in all matters of truth. He actually comforts and uplifts us in times of trouble and despair. Our only job is to invite the Holy Spirit into our hearts and allow Him to rule in our lives; this will cause us to prevail and be successful in life.

The bible also teaches us about the power of forgiveness. God instructs us to forgive one another as often as necessary. If we want God to forgive us, it is imperative that we forgive each other. As imperfect beings, we need God's forgiveness on a daily basis. The more we read and understand the bible, the more God continues to talk to us through His word. Reading the bible causes us to understand God's expectations of us. It also reminds us that He is always with us—we are never alone. God is always leading and guiding us in the right direction. It is up to us to listen, follow and obey.

Sometimes when we read God's word it seems as though a particular scripture is speaking directly to us. This scripture is actually ministering to us right where we are, in the midst of what we are dealing with or going through. It is as if a light comes on and everything becomes clear--making sense. You have a brand new revelation to a situation or problem. We are immediately uplifted because we have received the word we needed for that specific time or season in our lives. Many have described this reading experience as "the words literally seeming to be lifted or raised from the pages of the bible." This word or passage of scripture is called Rhema. It is a Rhema word because it is not just a casual or general reading of the scripture, but a reading that literally speaks to our specific situation. It is powerful and unforgettable. Oftentimes, individuals will attest to the fact that they have read a particular passage of scripture several times before, but it was not until that particular moment that the word spoke to them in a way that it had never spoken before; thus leaving an indelible impact which changes their lives forever.

There is so much that we learn about God, His plans and His promises when we read His word. As a result of reading His word, we also learn about ourselves. The word will expose and show us who we really are. It will convict us and bring about change in our lives, causing us to become better Christians. When we read God's word, we allow God to talk to us; informing us of how we should govern our lives.

### Preachers/Parents

God speaks to us through His preachers. Preachers who are truly called and are chosen by God have heard His voice. They have felt and heard God's urgings and promptings and responded to His call. When preachers walk with God as they should, by reading and studying God's word, fasting and praying, meditating and setting themselves apart to avail themselves to the leading and guiding of God, they will hear God speak to them. God uses many different means to speak to His preachers. Once the preacher receives the word from God, he is then able to give that word to the people. Moses, in the bible, was a prime example of one who received the word from the Lord and gave the word to the people.

When a preacher receives an appointment to preach to a certain congregation, he should seek to find out information about the church, its people and the purpose of the speaking engagement. If he is not asked to preach from a specific scripture or topic, then he should pray and listen for God to lead him to a scripture that will edify that particular body of Christ. God is omniscient. He knows who will be in attendance at the service and the message/word that the congregation needs to hear. It is imperative that the preacher keeps himself untangled and free from distractions so that he can hear clearly what God has to say to the church. Preaching is a serious matter and someone's life could be hanging in the balance just waiting for a word from God in order to make the right decision. The bible poses the question, "How can they hear accept from the preacher and how can he preach accept God sends him?"

It is important that we join a church where the word of God is being taught and preached. Everyone should have a pastor who is responsible for loving and praying for them. The pastor is responsible for caring for his members and going to God in prayer to receive the relevant, applicable word for the people. Not only should the pastor pray for his members but should also intercede on his members' behalf. The pastor's desire should be to see the sinner saved and the saved, growing and becoming more like Christ. Therefore, it is necessary for the pastor to seek God for the word that his congregation needs to hear. The pastor serves as a spiritual covering for the people who have joined his church and are following his lead. When we are connected to the right pastor, we will experience times in the service when it seems like our pastor is speaking specifically to us. It will seem as though he knows exactly what we are going through or dealing with at that particular time. This is because God is speaking through him so that he might speak to his members. That is why it is important for us to regularly attend the church that we have joined. The bible tells us not to forsake to assemble ourselves together. We are strengthened by the word that the pastor preaches. Additionally, we are strengthened by each other's testimony. If we are consistently staying home from church without good reason, we are failing to receive the word that God has for us. Thus, we are probably getting weaker spiritually, which means we are not growing stronger in our walk with God. Members who are saved but do nothing to feed or nourish their spirits begin to look more and more like the sinner who has never accepted Christ as their Savior. Just as it is necessary to feed our physical bodies with natural food, it is important that we feed our spiritual bodies with spiritual food--the word of God.

God also uses our parents/guardians and those who have rule over us to speak to us. The bible states that children should honor and obey their parents. In fact, the bible states that God rewards children who honor and obey their parents with long life. Parents refer to our natural or biological parents, adoptive parents, step-parents, as well as our spiritual parents. Those parents who love their children and are of sound minds will do everything they can to teach, protect, guide, instruct, encourage, nurture and support their children. They will only want and desire the best for their children and will do all in their power to ensure that their children's overall sense of health and well-being is not compromised.

I speak specifically to these parents because my experience as a licensed social worker has taught me that not all parents fit the bill and therefore, are either unable or unwilling to provide the loving, Godly care and instructions that their children need and deserve. However, we should strive to honor them anyway, even if for no reason other than the fact that they gave us life. We must remember that God did not indicate which parents deserved honor neither did He specify which children should honor their parents. He just said that children should honor their parents. I am sure that

God knew that all parents would not be deserving of honor when He gave us that command. However, we must keep in mind that the promise of long life is rewarded to the child for his/her obedience to God's command. Therefore, we must not allow anyone, even our parents, to cause us to jeopardize or forfeit God promises to us because of their negative or inappropriate behavior.

## Dreams

God also speaks to us through dreams. Dreams are a series of thoughts, pictures, or feelings that pass through the mind of a sleeping person. When God speaks through dreams, it affects our spirits and our souls. Godly dreams permeate our minds, our wills, and our emotions. Sometimes the pictures or the feelings in our dreams are so strong and vivid that when we wake up from the dreams, we can still feel its effects in the pit of our stomachs or the center of our hearts. This is a dream that cannot easily be shaken or forgotten. Somehow we know that this was not an ordinary dream. There is something different about this particular dream that causes an unrest that leads to an inward search for a deeper understanding or revelation.

Sometimes these dreams are so powerful that we are awakened in the midst of the dream; recalling vivid pictures and/or speaking aloud significant parts of the dream. Sometimes these dreams are recurrent. We may dream the same dream over and over again. Often times, we may not be able to make sense of the dream or ascertain its depth or true meaning. This is because when God speaks, He speaks volumes in just a few words or a few pictures. We have to consult God if we want to gain understanding. It does not matter how intelligent an individual may be or the number of degrees an individual might hold, man's intellect is no match for God. In fact, if we try to intellectualize what God is saying in the dreams, we are certain to arrive at the wrong interpretation.

The bible declares that God's ways are not our ways and His thoughts are not our thoughts. In fact, the Word tells us that our thoughts and God's thoughts are so different that it can be equated to the distance between heaven and earth. Scientists have determined that the earth is approximately 93,000,000 miles from heaven. With this fact in mind, clearly we should not rely on our own interpretation of dreams that have been sent by God. We should always pray and ask God to give us precise understanding of the dream. After all, if it is God who is speaking to us through the dreams, then He is more than capable of helping us to make sense of the dreams that we cannot figure out on our own. God will make the dreams clear to us so that we are able to get the messages that He is sending us. Our job is to seek God for the understanding. God is always willing and available to make things plain because it is His desire that we get the true meaning of His messages.

Although God speaks through dreams, we must be careful not to assume that all dreams come from God. Satan has a way of implanting some ungodly dreams in our spirits as well. Sometimes these unsolicited illicit dreams can evoke some of the same powerful responses as the Godly dreams. Again, we may wake up remembering or speaking aloud significant parts of the dream. However, we will know that these dreams are not from God because they do not line up with the word of God. If the dream is contrary to the word of God, then it was not from God. That's why it is important that we take the time to know God's Word. These ungodly dreams are not true, not pure and not just. If our dreams are not spiritually supported by the word of God, then we can safely assume that it was not from God.

Lastly, we might have some dreams that have nothing to do with God or Satan, but may be a direct result of the foods we ate, the movie we watched, or the thoughts we had the night before we fell asleep. We should not try to give more meaning or credence to the dream than is warranted because the dream could actually mean nothing. In fact, the bible warns us to tell a dream as a dream.

However, if we believe that God is speaking to us through a dream, we should meditate on it and pray about it before we go running to tell someone what we think God is saying. We should stand still and ask God for the explanation of the dream. Remember, if the dream is from God, it will be true and just and most importantly, it must be founded on biblical principles.

On the other hand, God sometimes gives us dreams to warn us or prepare us for future events. There are times when these dreams are difficult to understand because they are futuristic. We are not privy to the people or things we will encounter in our future. Only God knows the details of the path our future will take. Therefore, we must consult Him about these dreams. If God is preparing or warning us of a future event or person, He will often times show us the dream more than once. Each consecutive dream will bring a little more detail than the previous dream. We will not be able to shake the dream from our memories or thoughts. Again, this inability to move past the dream will cause us to seek God for the interpretation. We can be confident that God will help us to understand any dream that He gives us if we are willing to seek Him for clarity.

# Visions

God speaks through visions. Examples of visions are something seen in the mind; a dream seen while you are awake; a trance. Visions are a lot like dreams. We are able to see pictures or scenes of people or things in our minds. God often shows us visions while we are in prayer or deep meditation. If we are praying, then clearly we are awake. But oftentimes, we will have our eyes closed when we are talking to God. While talking to God in this manner, He will sometimes give us a vision about the thing we are praying about or the person we are praying for. This picture is vivid and profound. Like dreams, while the vision is very clear, there are times when we cannot figure it out. We see what we see. We know what we see, we can describe what we have seen to others, but we have no clue as to what it means. Again, this is the time to stay in prayer. We should ask God to explain, interpret or reveal the meaning of what we are seeing. If we ask God to clarify what we have seen, He will gladly do so. After all, He would not interrupt our prayer times with Him to show us a picture just for the sake of showing us a picture. There is a message He wants us to get and if we sit with Him long enough, we will get it.

God is showing us something that we were not aware of prior to the prayer experience. As I mentioned previously, God gives us messages/warnings through visions. The fact that God is showing us the vision is good in and of itself. Sometimes the content of the vision might not be good news but the fact that God is showing us allows us time to pray about the person/situation and to prepare for the situations/events by getting things in order. The fact that God is warning us or showing us things to come is an indication of His love and mercy towards us. Visions, like dreams, are not always sent to warn us of negative things to come. They sometimes occur to show us ourselves/others being promoted or elevated to where God is taking us. God sometimes gives us a glimpse of His plan for our lives. These visions help us to stay focused, motivated, and inspired to achieve the big plans that God has for our lives.

Sometimes the message of a vision may or may not be about us in particular, but it might be about a family member, colleague, or friend. Once God has made the vision clear to us, He might require us to share it with that individual.

If we are sincere in our prayer time, giving God our all, interceding and pouring out our hearts and souls to Him about a person or issue, and then we see a vision of the person or the thing we are praying about, we can safely assume that it is from God. However, we must wait for the clear, indisputable revelation of the vision before we attempt to say anything to anybody about what we think God might be saying to them. We must be clear about what God is saying. Too often, individuals are running around talking about what God said and God has not said anything. Please be cognizant of the fact that most of the time when God speaks to an individual, He is speaking to that person about their own situation. We must not be overly eager to tell other people what we think God is saying about them. Be extra careful when delivering messages to others from God. If God has given us the task of sharing the dream or vision, we will know it because God will not allow us to rest until it is done.

## Voice in Our Spirits

God will also speak to us in the inner parts of our beings; our spirits. There will be a voice that comes from the innermost part of us. A voice that is clear and concise. This voice is also profound and memorable. It always leaves us with a sense of peace, confidence and/or direction. God's voice is never jumbled or muffled. We never have to say, "Could you please repeat that?" We might be in awe of what we have heard, we might feel unworthy or puzzled about what we have heard, we may even be surprised about what we have heard; but we are sure about what we have heard and we know that it is the voice of God, especially when God is talking to us about ourselves. We cannot dispute what God says to us about us because He knows us better than we know ourselves. We must accept what God is saying. Oftentimes, God sees so much more in us then we are capable of seeing in ourselves.

Sometimes this inner voice provides us with the answers to questions we have posed to God in prayer. There are times we will hear the specific strategic plan as to how we should proceed in a situation. Sometimes we hear the prompting of God to remain silent or to simply be still, while there are other times we are prompted to speak up and take a stance. God speaks to us about our own issues (attitudes, lusts, biases, prejudices, jealousies, fears) that we may not be conscious of at the time. God enlightens us about these things so that we can address them. These are things we need to change, conquer and correct so that they do not serve as hindrances to the future plans that God has for our lives.

God's voice is unique. His voice is loving, yet stern and direct. He speaks eye–opening, jaw dropping truths about us. If we ask God a question, we must be prepared for His response. God has a way of answering our questions and telling us things about ourselves that will blow our minds and stop us in our tracks. He can "check us" or correct us in a single word or phrase that leaves us humbled and repentant. The only thing we can say is, "Okay God, I get it." No matter what it is that God tells us or reveals to us about ourselves, we quickly realize that we are always made better as a result of hearing His voice. But what really takes us over the top is our willingness and ability to hear, believe and obey what He says.

## Audible Voice

There are other times when God speaks audibly. This is when we hear the voice of God outside of ourselves. I believe that God speaks this way when He really needs to get our immediate attention. This voice is so clear, timely, concise and authoritative that the only thing we can do is accept what we have heard without question. This voice is so profound and life changing that it causes us to take action quickly. When God speaks audibly about us or our situations, we do not wonder if this is God, we know without a shadow of a doubt that it is Him. As a result, we will move quickly, and confidently to follow His instructions, being ever so grateful that we have developed a prayer relationship with Him that allows us to unmistakably recognize His voice. This voice is powerful! It does not matter what we are facing in our environments; it does not matter who believes or does not believe what we heard and know or if people think we are crazy, or look at us funny. This audible voice is not only clear and convincing, but it brings with it a type of urgency, excitement and anticipation for the thing that God has spoken and will bring to pass. It is a "yes and amen" situation and that settles everything. I get excited just thinking about this kind of experience. The audible voice sounds like your inner voice but louder!

## Signs

There are times when God will speak to us through signs. It is believed that the less mature Christian, who has not established a strong prayer life and routine devotional time for reading and studying God's word, will be more likely to rely on signs. These are Christians who have not experienced hearing the voice of God or may have heard His voice but did not recognize it to be the voice of God. It takes time, consistency, patience and perseverance to be able to clearly and confidently recognize God's voice.

The bible gives us a clear example of an individual, a babe in Christ, who did not recognize God's voice. This interesting and exciting story can be found in the first book of Samuel. There was a young man by the name of Samuel who loved God and was committed to His service but could not recognize God's voice. When Samuel heard God call his name, he ran to his spiritual leader to ask if he had called him. His leader informed him that he did not call his name. Samuel heard his name called again so he ran back to his spiritual leader a second time to ask him if he had called him. Again, the spiritual leader had not called Samuel. After hearing his name called again and running back to his spiritual leader to ask if he had called once more, the spiritual leader perceived that it was God who was calling him, so he instructed Samuel to acknowledge/respond to God the next time he heard his name called. Samuel did as he was instructed and was then able to receive the message that God had for him. Samuel learned that it was not his spiritual leader calling him but it was God.

Sometimes babes in Christ love the Lord, pray often, but have not yet developed the patience to persevere in prayer until they can hear and discern God's voice. So in their quest to know God's will, they will ask God to give them some kind of sign. They sincerely desire to know God's will before they make their moves or decisions. They resort to asking for a sign because they do not want to error in their ways and they truly want to know that what they are about to do is part of God's perfect will and plan for their lives.

For example, one might say, "God, if you really want me to pay tithes, let the preacher somehow mention the word tithe in his sermon this Sunday." If the preacher does mention the word tithe in his sermon, then the individual will take this as a sign that God wants him to pay tithes. On the other hand, if the preacher does not mention the word tithe in his sermon that Sunday, the individual might interpret it to mean that God does not want him to pay tithes. This faulty assumption could be totally avoided if this Christian was mature enough or disciplined enough to search the scriptures for God's will regarding tithing.

The other problem with relying on signs is we may get the sign we are asking for but we may sometimes still not be sure if it was a true sign from God. For example, we might believe that it was just a coincidence that the preacher mentioned the word tithe in his sermon. So we tend to say, "God if that really was a sign, then let the person who prays over the offering mention the word tithe. These scenarios can go on and on, until we have asked for about three different signs before we are convinced.

Other ways we might receive a sign from God is through a song on the radio, a bumper sticker on the back of a car, or a slogan from a poster or billboard. All these things might speak to us about our current situation and confirm or reiterate what we believe that God is conveying to us. Again, we must not overly rely on signs because if we are consciously looking for a sign to validate our beliefs, then we tend to see and hear what we want to hear because we want to see and hear it. It's kind of like falling in love with a particular car. Once we have decided that this is the car we want to purchase, it seems that this car happens to be everywhere we look. This is because we are preoccupied with the car, and not necessarily that it is a sign that God wants us to purchase that particular car.

Sometimes even the mature Christian might revert to asking God for a sign when they are in a jam and feel as though they need a quick answer from God. They too might become impatient and say, "God, please show me what you want me to do by letting this or that happen." However, they will not linger there with signs too long because they know and have experienced the real confidence, peace, and assurance that comes with knowing God's voice. The bible declares that God's sheep know His voice. Mature Christians will exercise the spiritual disciplines of prayer, reading God's word, meditation, and patience to hear what God is saying.

Please note that our maturity in Christ is not equated with how long we have been saved or call ourselves Christians, but rather how long we have been in an honest pursuit of God and His word. Maturity has more to do with our hunger and thirst for the gained knowledge and understanding of God and the disciplines we implement in our everyday lives to cultivate our spiritual relationships with Him.

**In Summary -** God is still speaking today. He speaks through His written word, the bible. When we read the bible, we are reading the Logos word of God. When the written word of God seems to jump off the pages or speak to us in a way that it has never spoken to us in the past, we are then experiencing the Rhema word of God. God is still calling men and women to preach the word of God. God uses these individuals as instruments to share the word He has given them for His people. Preachers and teachers are supposed to encourage and uplift the people of God. God also charges parents to speak words of truth, correction and encouragement to their children while He charges children to honor and obey their parents while under their care and supervision. God has promised to give long life to all children who keep His command.

God also speaks to us through dreams and visions. We must always be willing to tarry with God until He makes the dreams and visions clear. God also talks to us through the inner most parts of our spirits. He answers our prayers, drops words of wisdom and encouragement and correction in our inner beings/spirits so that we can grow and become more like Him. He might also talk in an audible voice that sounds much like our inner spirits. However, the sound will feel like it is outside of us and it has the capacity to cause us to look around to see who has spoken only to find that there is no one else in the room but us. Somehow we know that we have not lost our minds but we realize that our God has spoken!

Lastly, God will sometimes speak through signs. While asking God for a sign might be attributed to the less mature Christian, I believe that mature Christians sometimes revert to this practice from time to time. The goal however, is to strive to know God's voice in our hearts, audibly, in dreams and visions, through preachers, teachers and parents, and through His word. If one is to become confident in recognizing the voice of God, he must be willing to spend time in God's presence. Praying, reading, and studying God's word help us to develop the kind of relationship with God that aid us in knowing His voice. There will be times when we might miss His voice, or misunderstand His voice, but the more we develop our prayer life and study time, the better we will get at knowing His voice more precisely.

# Chapter 5 - Scriptures

1. For my thoughts are not your thoughts, neither are your ways my ways," declares the *LORD.* *Isaiah 55:8 NIV*

2. Honour thy father and mother; (which is the first commandment with promise;) *Ephesians 6:2 KJV*

3. In the last days, God says, I will pour out my Spirit on all people. Your sons and daughters will prophesy, your young men will see visions, your old men will dream dreams. *Acts 2:17 NIV*

4. For the flesh desires what is contrary to the Spirit, and the Spirit what is contrary to the flesh. They are in conflict with each other, so that you are not to do whatever you want. *Galatians 5:17 NIV*

5. My sheep hear my voice, and I know them, and they follow me *John 10:27 KJV*

# Chapter 6
# *Personal Testimonies of Hearing God's Voice*

# Chapter 6
# *Personal Testimonies of Hearing God's Voice*

### Praying for Nana

It was a cold night in the month of October in 1974. My dad and I went to church for the Friday Night Missionary Prayer Service. The rest of the family decided to take the night off; not me however. I loved going to church and I loved going to school... I rarely took a day off from either. If the church or school doors were open, I wanted to be there. I was always afraid that I might miss something good if I stayed home.

So, off we went to Highway church of Christ, located at 3100 West North Avenue, in Baltimore, Maryland. The late Bishop Fred Page Sr., was my pastor. It was a normal Friday night service. We began with a song and opening prayer, followed by testimonial service and the nightly offering. Then it was time for the preached word. On Fridays, the women preachers/missionaries were the featured speakers. We had what was called a platform service where we would hear from two to three speakers who had an opportunity to preach for fifteen to twenty minutes on a topic of their choice. At the age of 10, I had already accepted Jesus Christ as my personal Savior. At a young age, I always enjoyed getting a variety of sermons from the different speakers. I liked hearing and seeing the different preaching styles. I can still see those missionaries walking back and forth across the pulpit preaching the word of God. It was always a great time for me.

When it was time for prayer, we all gathered around the church altar to kneel down and pray. Once the altar was filled to capacity, we would spread out to the Mothers and Deacon Board pews. On this particular night, I was kneeling comfortably at the Mothers board pew. I enjoyed this part of the service also because it was a time when we could really take our time and pour out our hearts to God without any interruptions and there were no time restraints. We prayed aloud corporately and we did not stop until the last person was finished.

Since I was only twelve, I didn't have a whole lot to pray about, so I would often finish before everyone else. However, we were taught not to always rush back to our seats. We were taught to remain quiet and meditate for a while. We learned that if we stayed in the posture of prayer, maybe we would think of something or someone else to pray for. Thus, I would often stay still and listen to the older saints pray. My, oh my, could those saints pray. They seemed to never run out of words to say to God.

I remember one deacon in particular, Deacon Jimmie Thompson, Sr., who would always start out praying in

English, but before long he would start praying in his spiritual language. You could always hear the anointed power of the Holy Spirit when his prayer shifted to another level. His prayers always sounded like music to my ears. I can remember listening and waiting for his spiritual prayer language (speaking in tongues) to take over. I was never disappointed because it happened every time he prayed. I can remember wanting to be able to pray in tongues like him one day. Since I was only twelve, I figured the tongues would come in time. So, in the meantime, I stuck to what I knew – English!

I had been attending these services for several years now. So, I do not want to paint this rosy picture that represents this little girl who always enjoyed every night of these prayer services. There were a few times when I could not wait to be done with all of this praying. Sometimes my knees would get sore from kneeling so long. There were times when I wished the more seasoned saints didn't have so much to pray about. I can remember saying to myself, "Come on missionary so and so, it's time to go home; please don't start up again!" There were other times when I would just make myself comfortable and drift off to sleep. I would wake up when my pastor would start singing a song, which signaled to us that prayer time was coming to an end. Sometimes I would say, "Thank You Jesus!" No one could have ever imagined how happy I was to hear my Bishop sing.

On Friday evenings, after church service, my family would stop at the Chinese Joint, Harry Little Submarine Shop and Arundel Ice Cream Shop. These three eateries had the best Chinese food, submarines, and ice cream in the city. At any rate, all of these early prayer experiences were pivotal to my spiritual development--I would not trade them for anything. In fact, a smile rushes across my face every time I reminisce about those wonderful spirit-filled times we had at

Highway Church of Christ. The Friday night Missionary Prayer services were pivotal spiritual experiences for me as a child. They taught me how to pray and how to believe and trust God. I learned how to be still, meditate, wait and listen. This was a time when prayer services were authentic; where the seasoned saints would get into the presence of God, praying until things changed. This was a time when the deacons and the mothers of the church would tell you such things like, "Just talk to Jesus; tell Him all about your troubles," or "Take your burdens to the Lord and leave them there," and "He may not come when you want Him but He is right on time." This early prayer experience was priceless and it served as a launching pad that sparked in me an earnest desire to pray, trust and believe God for solutions to all of my prayers.

It was on this cold October evening that I began to say my prayers as usual. However, I soon would learn that there was nothing usual about this prayer service. The order of the service was the same, but my prayer experience was different. There was no finishing early and listening to others pray. There was no waiting to hear my pastor sing the closing song and there definitely was no sleeping! This time, I prayed all the way to the end of our prayer time and when we were done, I was almost too weak to stand up and return to my seat. I had experienced something that I had never experienced before. I had a vision. I had heard people speak, preach and teach about visions, but I had never experienced one myself. It was something that I will never forget as long as I live.

During my prayer time, I began to pray for Nana, my maternal grandmother. This was nothing new or unusual. I always prayed for her. I would ask God to save her, bless her and protect her. She was a wonderful grandmother who enjoyed spending time with her grandchildren. She had a kind heart and a loving spirit. She had such a warm presence that even our neighborhood friends would call her Nana, as we did. Nana was also funny and always knew how to make us laugh. However, Nana had not accepted Christ as her personal Savior. I understood, at an early age, that being a good person does not qualify one for eternal rest with God. Therefore, I always prayed for her salvation.

On this particular night, while praying for my grandmother, I was shocked by a vision of her lying in a casket. It was like a dream, but I was awake and I could not believe what I was seeing. My heart started pounding and I began to weep profusely. I cried as I asked God to please spare her life; give her more time as I knew she needed time to accept Him as her personal Savior. I pleaded with God to give me a chance to talk with her about the importance of being saved. After a while, the picture changed from her lying in a casket to her sitting up smiling in her living room chair. Immediately, I knew that God had answered my prayer. I knew that God had spared her life. Crying tears of joy, I thanked God for hearing and answering my prayer.

It was an awesome thing to know that an Almighty God would answer the prayer of a twelve-year-old girl. This prayer convinced me of God's love for me as well as His ability and willingness to hear and answer prayers. You cannot imagine how grateful I was to God. It was as if I had just witnessed my grandmother's funeral. My eyes were puffy and red. I remember a friend hugging me and asking me what was wrong. Of course, I could hardly begin to articulate what I had just experienced. How could I explain that I had just seen a vision of my grandmother dead, but now I knew she was still alive?

When church was over, I caught up with my dad and I said, "Dad, you would not believe what happened to me tonight!" I told him about my vision during our ride home. He said "WOW! That was some experience." He said, "You know you are going to have to tell your mother about this. I don't know how she is going to take it, but you will have to tell her." I said, "Yes, I know." Seemingly, thousands of thoughts and questions began to flood my mind. What would my mother say? Would she believe me? Would she be angry? Would she be sad? Would she cry? Maybe she would think I was crazy. How was I going to tell her what I had seen while in prayer? I knew it had to be done despite my fear and anxiety about her reaction. At least I was glad to be able to tell her that I knew her mother was still alive because she was sitting up in her living room chair smiling at the end of the vision.

Thankfully, she was receptive as she listened to me tell her the vision. She asked me to repeat it again as I knew she was saddened by the news, yet grateful that God had extended more time to her mother. She said, "Okay, you know we will have to tell your grandmother about this, don't you?" I said yes but I was afraid and really did not want to tell her but I knew I had to. She said, "Yes, you have to tell her but I will be there with you." My mother called my grandmother and told her that we would be coming to visit with her tomorrow as we had something important to discuss with her. Of course she wanted to know what it was about, but my mother said, "Everything is okay. We will talk to you on tomorrow."

Saturday afternoon we saw my grandmother and began our visit as normal with hugs and kisses. Later, my mom set the stage for me to tell my Nana the vision. I told her about the vision. Surprisingly, she was actually sitting in the chair smiling at me just as she was in the vision. After hearing the vision, she was not upset, she was not distressed and she did not even seem to be sad or fearful. In fact, she somewhat corroborated the vision by telling us that she knew something was happening because she kept having dreams of her deceased relatives. She stated that these relatives came to her and called her by name. She began to tell my mother and I specific dreams she had recently of deceased family members. I could not believe how well she was taking the news.

Later, my mother talked to her about accepting Christ as her Savior. She agreed and said she was willing to do so, but she let us know that she did not think she could go to church as often as we did. We both laughed and told her that it was okay if she didn't attend as often as we did. My mother told her that everything would be okay if she accepted Jesus Christ as her Savior and came to church as often as she could. We would be sure to pick her up whenever she wanted to go. Eventually my grandmother went to church and gave her life to Christ. She really enjoyed fellowshipping with the members of the church.

Approximately three months later, my grandmother passed away peacefully in her sleep.
Although my mother was devastated, she was glad that her mother had accepted Christ before she died. We were all saddened by our loss. There was no one more loving, free-spirited and funny as Nana. My dad was extremely sad too because she truly was like a mother to him.

### How Did God Speak?

God spoke through a vision. In the midst of my prayer, I saw a real life picture as if I was watching a film or having a dream. However, I was fully awake. In this vision, God showed me an event that was about to take place. I saw my grandmother lying in a casket. I prayed and asked God to extend her time and He did; allowing her to live long enough to accept Him as her Lord and Savior. The next scene in the vision was a picture of my grandmother sitting up smiling in her living room chair. This second picture was confirmation that God had answered my prayer

## The Car of My Dreams

It was a clear and sunny afternoon when my dad and I went out again to find the car of my dreams. I had fallen in love with the 1983 red, four-door, Nissan Sentra. It was pretty! It was a shiny fire engine red with a light grey interior. I would smile every time I saw someone driving down the street in one. "That's my car!" I would say and, "That's the color!" Although the Nissan Sentra came in a variety of different colors, none of the colors looked as good as the red one to me. There was something about that shiny red and that light grey interior that made me know that this was the car for me!

My dad and I had gone out several times, visiting several car dealerships. All of the dealerships had the Sentra, but they either did not have the color or they did not have the four-door model. When I think back on my age at the time, I wondered why I was so stuck on having a four-door car. I mean what young college student cares if the car has two doors or four? I guess it was because my dad always bought four door cars to ensure that there was easy access for any adult who needed a ride. At any rate, the car had to be red and it had to have four doors.

Unfortunately, we had exhausted all of our options and could not find that particular car. My dad and the salesperson tried to get me to consider changing the color, but I would not because no other color would suffice. It had to be red. Many of the salesmen called to other dealerships, but according to them, everyone had sold out of the red Sentras. One salesperson said he had checked everywhere and there weren't any red Sentras left in the entire country. My dad and I laughed about that statement. We said that this salesman really wanted to make the sale by convincing me to choose another color. We figured that there was no way he could actually know if the entire country was sold out of red, four door, Nissan Sentras. So, we continued to search every dealership we could find, but we had no luck. We were beginning to think that maybe that salesperson was right. We went back home again without a car.

My dad said, "Daughter, I think you are going to have to decide on a different color Sentra or a different model red car." I was inclined to believe him because everywhere we went, we were hearing the same things: "We have the car but it is not red" or "We have the red car but it is not a four door." I agreed that I would be more flexible the next time we went out. I tried hard to talk myself into liking the burgundy Sentra. I realized that I needed to like a different color before we went out on our next car shopping adventure. However, before I totally gave in, I decided to pray about it. So, Friday night I seriously prayed about this car. I said, "God, if there is a red, four door, Nissan Sentra out there somewhere, please help us find it tomorrow." I figured if anybody knew what was out there, it would be God. I put my specific request in His hands and prayed myself to sleep.

That night, I had a dream that there was a red, four door, Nissan Sentra located at Bob Bell's Nissan on Eastern Avenue. The identifying factor about this red Sentra was a small cigarette burn in the driver's seat. It was not a big deal, just a small hole. When I woke up Saturday morning, I told my dad that I had a dream about the car. I told him that there was a red Nissan Sentra located at Bob Bell's on Eastern Avenue. "But we have already been there," he said. "I know," I said. "But we have got to go back there because I saw the Bob Bell sign and I saw a cigarette burn in the driver's seat of the car." He smiled and gave me a raised eyebrow look, but said, "Okay, we will go back there again." So off we went down the road to Bob Bell's Nissan. Once again, we met a salesman who told us that the only red Sentra they had on the lot was a two door. My father suggested that we should take a look at it. I looked at it and I said, "This is not the car because there is no cigarette hole in the driver's seat." We walked around some more because I was determined to find that car. Finally, we gave up and proceeded to walk off the lot when someone pulled up in a red Sentra. My heart started pounding. I said, "Dad, here comes a red Sentra!" From a distance, it looked like a two door. We stopped in our tracks and watched as the family who had just test drove the car pulled right in front of us and parked. It was a red, four door Nissan Sentra!!! I was so excited that I did not know what to do with myself. My father asked me to calm down because we needed to find out from the salesman if the person was interested in purchasing the car. The family got out of the car. My dad waited patiently to talk to the salesman, but I ran around to check out the driver's seat. I was looking for the tiny little cigarette hole. There it was! Just like it was in the dream. I ran back to my father and said, "This is it, this is my car; come and look at the cigarette hole in the driver's seat!" My dad was amazed. Of course the family decided not to purchase the car. How could they? It was already mine. God showed it to me in a dream the night before. Only God could have allowed this to happen!

We finally made it to the salesman's desk. Now my dad was doing what men do to get the price right. The salesperson was running back and forth to his supervisor like car salesmen do. After some time, I started to get tired. The next time the salesman left to consult with his supervisor about the price, I leaned over to my father and said, "Dad, you do know that that is my car out there and we are not leaving here without it, so you all need to close this deal." He laughed and said, "I know that but he doesn't, just sit tight." I took a deep breath and sat back in my chair. My dad put his serious face back on and they haggled for a little while longer and then finally it was over. My dad got the deal he wanted and I got to drive off the lot in the exact car of my dreams!

## How Did God Speak?

God spoke in a dream. I prayed before I went to sleep about this car. I asked God to let us find the red, four door, Nissan Sentra the next day, if this car was available. I went to sleep and had a dream about the car that night. In the dream, God revealed the name of the dealership, the location, and an identifying mark which would signify the exact car I saw in my dream; a small insignificant cigarette burn on the driver's seat. It is amazing to know that God hears and answers our prayers even when it is not a terribly important request. God's word declares that He will supply our needs, but I learned that sometimes He will also give us exactly what we want!!!

## Keeping Me Safe from Unseen Danger!!!

After a long night of studying, at Cook Library, on the campus of Towson State University, I began packing up my books to leave the library to go home. I was especially excited that evening because for the first time, I would be driving myself home. There was no need for me to call anyone to pick me up because I had just purchased my first car the weekend prior. It was a spanking brand new red 1983 Nissan Sentra. It was my junior year of college and I was driving the car of my dreams.

After packing up my books, I smiled as I pulled out my keys and proceeded to exit the library. Just as I entered the final corridor to exit the building, I heard a voice that said, "Call Angelo to pick you up." I said, "Not tonight, you drove yourself to school today, remember?" I easily dismissed the voice because I figured that it was only out of habit that I thought to call Angelo for a ride home. I smiled to myself as I proudly walked down the library steps heading into the direction of the parking lot. I heard the voice again. It said the same thing, 'Call Angelo to pick you up." I stopped in my tracks, looked around, paused for a while and then decided to return to the library. I walked back inside the library's corridor, sat on the bench, stared at the pay phones in the hallway, and said, "Why should I call my fiancé to pick me up when I drove myself to school?" This just did not make any sense at all. Besides, he would probably think I had lost my mind as he knew how excited I was to be driving my new car to school today. After sitting on the bench for a while, contemplating what to do, I decided that maybe I just needed to be cautious. I would wait for the next crowd of students who were leaving the library and walk with them. More than likely, someone in the crowd would be walking towards the Administrative Building parking lot where my car was parked. I figured that everything would be okay. And I would be safe as long as I kept up with the crowd.

I waited for a while and then off I went with the next crowd of students. We had gone about half a block when suddenly I heard the voice a third time, "Call Angelo to pick you up." I looked at the crowd of students I had been walking with, none of whom I knew. However, they all looked like normal, harmless students, who had no reason to hurt me. Once again, I shook it off. I ignored the voice and kept walking when suddenly I heard the voice one more time. It was louder and even more forceful than the other times. It said the same thing, "Call Angelo to pick you up!" I felt my body trembling with fear. I quickly returned to the library and sat on the bench to compose myself. I looked at my watch, looked at the pay phones and decided to call Angelo. I felt stupid, but I made the call. I began with the regular small talk, "What are you doing?" "How was your day etc.?" Then I said, "I know this sounds crazy because it's crazy to me, but I need you to come and pick me up at the library and drive me across the street to my car." I explained that I had attempted to leave the library several times, but I kept hearing this voice which directed me to call him. I explained that I could no longer ignore what I perceived to be the voice of God.

Without any questions or hesitation, he said, "Okay, stay where you are. I will be there to get you." At this point, the librarian was making her first closing announcement. I watched as a few straggling students exited the library. I shook my head thinking, "I could have been home by now." About 15 minutes later, the librarian announced that the library was now closed. The staff was now turning off the lights and leaving the building.

The custodian, who saw me sitting alone on the bench, asked if I were okay as he was about to lock the front doors. I stated that I was fine and was waiting on my ride. As we walked out together, he asked me if I were sure I would be okay and offered to wait with me until my ride arrived. I assured him that I would be okay. I sat down on the bench outside of the library and suddenly Angelo pulled up. The custodian smiled, we waved goodbye and I got into the car. I was so relieved and thankful when I saw Angelo pull up. I shook my head and laughed about how crazy this whole ordeal was. It felt silly for me to ask him to drive 40 minutes in order to drive me approximately 5 minutes to my own car.

As we drove to the first parking lot, we saw that there were still a few cars scattered throughout the lot. Then we drove to the bottom lot where we were shocked to find that there was only one car left in the entire bottom lot--mine. My red Nissan Sentra was parked about four feet away from the wooded area of the lot. Then, I said to Angelo, "Maybe this is why I needed you to bring me here so that I would not have to walk down the steps, in the dark by myself, to the only car left in the bottom lot." He said, "Yes that was probably the reason you needed to call me." At that moment, I realized that I would have walked safely to the first lot where the other students had parked, but I still would have had to walk alone to the second parking lot where my car was parked.

I was relieved that I had finally listened to the voice. Angelo proceeded towards my car. The headlights were shinning bright when suddenly, we saw a man jump up from the driver's side of my car door and ran into the woods. He was stooped down by my door! I could not believe my eyes. I looked at my fiancé and asked, "Did you see that? Did I really just see a man run away from my car into the woods?" He said, "Yes, I saw him." My heart was pounding. Now everything made sense as we sat in disbelief. Chills shook my body while tears ran down my face. I could only imagine what I might have experienced had I not harkened to the voice of God. Tears streamed down my face even more as I thought of the loving and persistent voice of God. My heavenly father was speaking to me; telling me to do what did not make sense to me. He knew that my life was in danger and He was trying to keep me safe. We sat there for a few minutes until I got myself together. My fiancé saw me safely into my car and then he followed me all the way to my home.

Approximately one week later, the University announced that there was a rapist in the vicinity. A young lady had reported that she had been raped on the grounds of Towson State University's campus. I knew if I had not heard and obeyed the voice of God, that young lady would have been me a week earlier. Every time I think about it, every time I tell this story, I shudder to think about what could have happened to me that night. I think about how my life would have been impacted, how my relationship with my husband, might have been affected. I wonder how many times I would have beaten myself up for not listening to the voice of God. There would have been no one to blame but myself. Even now, with tear filled eyes, I thank God for speaking to me again and again that night. He was directing me, no—He demanded that I make that call!

### How Did God Speak?

God spoke in dreams. Prior to the above incident occurring, I had several unexplainable dreams. In the dream, I saw myself standing in a crowd of people who appeared to be my friends. I was in the crowd with friends but I felt unsafe. I felt like I was about to be raped. I never saw anyone approach or attack me and I never saw the rape occur, but I felt like it was about to happen. I woke up from the dream thinking that the dream was weird. Why was I standing comfortably in the crowd but feeling unsafe? I felt somewhat disturbed by the dream but I could not make sense of it, so I dismissed it and decided that this was just another crazy dream.

About a week later, I had the same dream. I was standing in a crowd of people who appeared to be friends; yet I had this terrible feeling that someone was going to rape me. I woke up scared because this was the second time I had this dream. I thought about where I might be with a group of

116

people. After much thought, I figured that I would most likely be at church or at school. I felt safe in both places. I thought about all of the friends I hung out with. I could not imagine that any of my male friends would harm me. This was very disturbing to me. I shared this dream with one of my best friends, Rosemary. I met her at Towson University and learned that she attended the church of another one of my best friends, Laura. I was the connection between the two of them. The three of us continue to be friends to this day.

I was surprised to learn that Rosemary had the same dream that I had. However, she felt like she was about to be raped. We quickly realized that this was no coincidence but a warning from God. Neither of us could figure out why we would be amongst friends and feel like a rape was about to occur. We could not make sense of the dream but we agreed that we must always stay in a crowd and never go anywhere alone. Even more importantly, we began to earnestly seek God for his protection. We agreed to stay in prayer; asking God to cover us with His blood and to keep us safe from seen and unseen danger. We prayed that no harm would come to either of us. We thanked God for the warning dreams but asked for clarity as we could not figure out the people in the crowd. It was not until after the incident that the dream began to make sense. The night I attempted to leave Cook Library, I was walking with students with harmless and friendly faces. I would have been safe walking with the crowd to a certain point. We would have all gotten to parking lot A, but I would have had to walk to parking Lot B alone. Because none of these students were actually friends of mine, I would not have asked them for a ride to my car.

I would have had a false sense of safety walking with them to the parking lot until I saw that everyone in the crowd was parked in the first lot. They would have gotten into their cars and driven off while I would have had to walk to the bottom lot where the rapist was waiting to attack me.

God used two ways to communicate with me regarding this impending rape. First, He spoke to me through several unexplainable dreams, and then He spoke to me from the inner recesses of my spirit. The voice was consistent, clear and persistent. His voice saved me from rape and possibly death. I am so glad that I was able to hear and finally obey the voice of the Lord. God knows that I am eternally grateful for His divine protection.

## The Storm

I was about to leave college to go home. However, it was forecasted that a severe storm was approaching our city. There were strong winds, thunder and lightning and heavy down pours of rain. The sky was grey and this forecast was really bleak as the meteorologists announced that this would be one of the biggest thunderstorms in recent times. They warned people to stay inside and take shelter; venture out only if it was absolutely necessary.

I pondered whether to stay at school and wait for the storm to pass or take my chances and brave the storm in order to make it home. After giving it some thought, I decided to venture out into the storm; praying the entire time until I made it safely home. I was not really afraid to be in the storm, but I really did not like hearing the thunder or seeing the lightening flashing. The thunder was so loud that it seemed like it shook the ground while the lightening, with all of its brightness, lit up entire city blocks. I was in awe of the strong winds that shook the cars, turned over porch furniture, and caused a whirlwind of trash and other debris to race up and down the streets. This storm caused traffic signs to fall, wires to hang and traffic lights to swing. I had never seen so many trees that were once standing tall now uprooted from the ground; tree branches and leaves were everywhere. I could not help but think about and revere the power of God as I witnessed the impact of this unforgettable storm.

As I continued to pray and drive, I noticed a humongous tree that was located about a block ahead of me. My eyes were fixed on this tree because of its massive size and height. The width and length of the tree was immense. This tree stood a good distance from the curbside of the street. It looked robust and sturdy as it stood tall and erect; hovering boldly over the other trees that had fallen. I was fascinated by it. I imagined that this tree must have been around for a long time and must have seen many storms. I realized that the bark and the height of this tree was indicative of how far down its roots were embedded. Therefore, the size and height of the tree, which captured my attention above ground, was merely a mirror of what was going on below ground. Surely this tree had stood the test of time. I thought to myself, "Not even lightening could bring this tree down." I smiled to myself as I approached the tree. "Yeah, this old tree will still be standing when the storm is over. Once I was really close up to the tree, I heard God's voice. MOVE!!!! Instantly, I stepped on the gas and moved into the other lane. I was in utter shock and disbelief as I watched that humongous tree that I thought was unmovable fall in my rear view mirror. There was a loud thump as the biggest tree I had ever seen hit the ground, covering the entire two-lane street. I could not believe what had just happened. It felt like I was in a twilight zone or a badly scripted movie scene.

If I were watching what had just happened in a movie, I would have said that the scene was poorly scripted because there was no way that the driver would have known that that particular tree would fall. And to make matters worse, how would he know precisely when to move, with what speed to get out of harm's way? If I were viewing this scene in a movie, I would have said that the script was not realistic because in real life, that driver would have been smashed under the tree. But I was not watching a movie and what I was experiencing was real. Everything happened so quickly. I had no time to think, analyze or question the voice. In fact, it seemed as if God shouted MOVE!!! Pushed the gas pedal, and swerved the stirring wheel all at the same time.

Clearly, there are no words to explain how I felt. Once the tree fell, the entire street was shut down. The huge tree covered the two-lane street, bringing all the cars in both lanes to a screeching halt. I was in total shock as I replayed what had just happened in my mind. I wondered what the drivers, who were stopped at the red light, were thinking. They must have said to themselves, "How did she know to move out of the way?" The only thing I could do was shake my head in amazement and disbelief. I knew that I was serving an awesome God. Only God could have had my eyes fixed on that tree from a distance and shout MOVE at the exact moment that it would fall. Only God! In that very moment, I knew without a shadow of a doubt, that God loved me. He was an awesome protector then and He is still my protector today. I thanked Him for His divine protection as I drove the rest of the way home.

## How Did God Speak?

First, God spoke through a sign. He showed me the tree and allowed me to become enthralled with it because of its size, or so I thought. I later learned that I was captivated by it because it was an impending danger to my life. Right in the nick of time, I heard God's voice audibly. I heard His voice clearly and urgently. The voice was so crisp, loud, and urgent that it immediately grabbed my attention. God knew that once my car reached a certain proximity to the tree, I needed to move quickly away from the humongous tree that I once thought was unmovable. My car was the last car to pass that tree that evening. I passed it safely because I heard God's voice; the only one who could have known precisely when, how, and in what direction, that tree would fall. Only God!

## Prophecy – A spiritual Gift

We probably have all heard, at one time or another, that we were created for a purpose; created to solve a problem, improve economic and social conditions, tear down racial barriers, promote equality, fight for justice, educate and inspire our youth, empower and advocate for the poor, the frail, and the sick. Maybe we were created to start a business, preach a sermon, rear, nurture and protect our children, write a book or the lyrics to a song. Most of us have heard, over and over again, that we were not created out of happenstance or mistake, even if our births were unplanned. Only God can create life and it is He who has a plan for the life He gives us.

So, with all of that in mind, I decided one Saturday afternoon, to seek God for my purpose. I always had a sneaking suspicion that I would be doing something in the church like preaching, but of course, that was not what I wanted to do. I really wanted to sing. I wanted to be able to belt out a song and set the church on fire. I figured singing would not require too much accountability. Singing would not cause others to expect more from me than the average church member. The most others would say is, "Wow, she really has a beautiful voice" or maybe they would say, "She is an anointed singer." I figured I could handle that much attention. Do not misunderstand me, I was always serious about my salvation and I had no intention of bringing shame to God or the body of Christ.

However, at that time, I really believed that the preacher had to be absolutely perfect without any room for error. And that expectation seemed to be too awesome a charge to keep, even for me, who loved the Lord with all my heart, mind, and soul. I really believed that God only called perfect people to ministry. I did not realize that God called ordinary people to do extraordinary things because of His power and not their own power. And while there is and should be a greater burden to honor and respect the call of God on one's life, I now know and understand that forgiveness is made available to the preacher just as it is for those who sit in the pew. God knows that none of us are perfect. That is precisely why He sent His son. I know this now, but I did not fully understand it when I was seeking Him for my purpose.

I was in my late twenties. My husband was out of the house and I had just put my baby girl, Courtney, to sleep in her crib. It seemed like a perfect time to pray without distractions. I took my bible with me to the living room, placed it on the chair in front of me where I knelt to pray. I prayed with much sincerity, asking God to please show me my gift or purpose. After I finished praying, I picked up the bible and randomly turned to a place in the bible, hoping that I would land on the word that God wanted me to know.

I turned to the 33rd chapter of Ezekiel. This scripture spoke about Ezekiel being a watchman unto the house of Israel. The watchman was charged with the duty of blowing the trumpet to warn the people when the sword of the Lord was against them. This scripture made it clear that if the people heard the warning and changed their ways, then they would be delivered. However, if they heard the warning and failed to change their ways then they would be forced to deal with the consequences. Their blood would be upon their own heads. However, this scripture warned Ezekiel that if he failed to warn the people of impending danger, thus preventing them the opportunity to make changes, then their blood would be charged to his hand.

Oh NO!!! I slammed the bible shut, jumped up from my knees, ran to put the bible back where I had gotten it from and said to God, "You must have gotten me mixed up with someone else; there is no way I am going to be a prophetess!" I told God, "I was too young and I surely did not have the spiritual depth needed to have this kind of gift." My heart was racing and I could hardly wait for my husband to get back home so that I could tell him my experience. After sharing my experience with him, I told him that I knew that I had gotten the wrong message. I knew that particular scripture reading was just a fluke and really had nothing to do with me as an individual; therefore, I was not going to worry about this experience anymore. And that is exactly what I did.

I literally blocked this prayer experience from my mind. This experience was so traumatic to me that I did not remember it until years later. Because of my expertise in the field of Psychology, Sociology, and Social Work, I understand that I had experienced what is called repressed memory. Repressed memory is often what happens to young children who have experienced traumatic events in their childhoods. Oftentimes, children who have been victims of physical and/or sexual abuse, adopt this coping mechanism to literally block their negative experiences from their minds. This allows them to continue to function as normal as possible in an abnormal living environment. It usually takes hypnosis and/or years of psychotherapy to unravel these unconscious traumatic experiences.

It's amazing to think how afraid I was of this gift. My earliest recollection of prophetesses in the church, were that of much older, spiritually seasoned, women who always dressed in long white dresses. I would see these women when we went to Florida in the month of May, for our general convention. They always seemed to be prophesying gloom and doom. They would give a word of correction to the church and sometimes they would call out specific people to warn them individually. We would come back to the convention the following year and learn that everything they said actually happened. I could remember being very scared and nervous when these women spoke. No, No, No!!! I was not going to be that person. I did not want people to be afraid of me like I was afraid of those women in white. So, yep… I blocked the whole thing out of my mind.

Several years later, my pastor, the late Bishop Fred Page Sr., had a service where he laid hands on members of the church in an effort to stir up the spiritual gifts that God had placed in them. Many of these gifts were lying dormant in the church. I was not at this service, but I heard about how God had really used the pastor to stir up gifts in the saints. I was so upset that I had missed that service. I cannot remember why I was not there that night but I kept beating myself up for being absent. Shortly thereafter, I decided that I would seek God for myself. I knew that I was supposed to be doing something in the Kingdom and I told God that I was ready to find out what it was. I asked him to reveal my gift to me. I prayed and I meditated because I was tired of not knowing what my gift was. I prayed earnestly throughout the day, seeking God for an answer, but I did not get an answer that day.

I got up early Sunday morning in anticipation of getting myself ready for church. As I sat on the side of the bed, I closed my eyes and said, "Lord I am ready to know what my gift is." Immediately, I saw a vision of myself kneeling in the living room of the house I used to live in years ago, with the bible in my hand. Everything came rushing back to my memory. I remembered the prayer and the scripture. I remembered telling God He had made a mistake and had gotten me confused with someone else. I wept. My husband asked me what was wrong but I could hardly get it out. I could not believe that God had been so patient with me. And several years later, He was still saying the same thing He had told me years earlier. God had already told me that I had the gift of prophecy, but I was not ready to receive it. What was so amazing and humbling for me, is that God did not hold it against me. What an awesome God!

I went to church that Sunday morning. It was the third Sunday of the month and my choir, The Inspirations of Highway, was singing that Sunday. The only thing I can say is, "We had church!" The young people's choir sang under the power and anointing of God. The spirit fell down and the church went up in a mighty praise. We danced until we could dance no more. Choir chairs were everywhere. We finally were able to re-organize the chairs back to their original places so that we could settle down to hear the preached word of God.

After the benediction, as I was coming down from the choir stand, I was stopped by Sister Shannon, a dear friend of my family and a faithful member of the church. She said, "Sister Mims, I was watching you this morning and the spirit of God was all over you. You must do what God is telling you to do, whatever it is, you must surrender." All I could say was, "I know, I know you are right and I am surrendering." With tears streaming down my face, I continued to proceed towards my seat when I was stopped again by a regular visitor, Sister Brown, who was recently married to a Deacon of our church. She walked up to me and said, "Prophecy, I see it all over you. God says you must tell it in season and out of season. Tell it if they want to hear it and if they do not want to hear it, and do not be afraid of their faces." Once again, all I could say was, "Yes, yes, yes." I could barely stand up as I was so weak from the power of God I felt that day. There was nothing else to be said. God had already spoken to me that morning, reminding me of an earlier prayer experience. God showed me a vision of myself praying to Him years earlier, asking Him to tell me my gift. God also confirmed this vision a couple hours later at the church, through the words of Sis. Shannon. Then He confirmed it again through the words of Sister Brown; back to back. Everything was settled. Clearly, there was nothing else to be said. I knew what God wanted me to know and now I was able to accept it. From that point on, my prayer was, "Not my will Lord, but thy will be done."

### How Did God Speak?

God spoke through prayer, the Bible, a vision and two women of God, to ensure that I got His message. Several years prior, I had prayed for God to reveal my gift to me. I received the answer immediately following prayer as I turned to a particular passage of scripture. The scripture identified the role of the prophet. Clearly, I was not able to receive what God had revealed to me, at that time. I had literally forgotten about that prayer experience. Years later, I was asking God the same question that I had asked Him previously. God showed me a vision of myself on my knees, receiving the answer the first time. The prayer experience and the vision of that prayer experience happened many years apart. This was a clear indication that God does not change His mind about what He has called us to do.

## God Knows My Heart

One Saturday afternoon, I gathered my bills from the kitchen drawer, took my checkbook out, and began to pay my bills, as normal. I sat there for a while and then decided that I would not pay my tithes this time. After all, my husband was laid off from work. He was now collecting an unemployment check, which was no comparison to his regular paycheck. Therefore, I decided to explain to God why I was making the decision to not tithe this time. I knew what the word said about 10% of our earnings belonging to God, but I believed I had a good reason to stop for a short while. I knew it would only be temporary as I knew my husband would be back to work within a reasonable amount of time.

My husband worked as an Iron Worker, thus his work was seasonal. It also was transient in that he moved from one location to another; staying on one job for as long as it took to get the job completed. He helped to build stadiums, banks, bridges, hospitals, world trade centers, tunnels and other buildings in downtown Baltimore, (MD), around the city, county and surrounding areas. Once a job was completed, it was typical for him to be laid off if additional work was not readily available. Therefore, being laid off was not as significant or alarming in his line of work as it might have been in other jobs or career fields. I believed that a temporary reprieve from tithing would not be a big deal as I would go right back to tithing as soon as he got his next job. This was my solution for helping our money to stretch further. My newly developed plan was to tithe while he was working and stop tithing when he was laid off.

It seemed like a logical, well thought out plan to me. I figured that everything would be just fine; after all God knew my heart! He knew that I wholeheartedly believed in the principle of tithing. Both of my parents were tithers and they taught us this biblical principal at an early age. I can remember proudly putting my first 50 cents into the tithing envelope. I was grinning from ear to ear when I took my tithing envelope to the offering table. The tithing envelopes looked different from the regular offering envelopes. I felt like a grown up because I was finally able to put money in the tithing envelope. I could hardly wait until Sunday morning to pay 10% of the $5.00 I had earned scrubbing and waxing my neighbor's porch.

I took this opportunity to proudly remind God of how long I had been tithing. I wanted God to understand that I truly believed in the tithing principle, but I just could not afford to tithe at this time. I explained that our two checked family income had decreased as a result of my husband being laid off, but our bills remained the same. Therefore, I decided that I would use the tithe money to help with the bills. After all, this is what teamwork is all about; it was me having his back like he has mine. I really wanted God to understand that this was not an act of disobedience, but I really could not afford to tithe at this time.

Just as I finished what I thought was an excellent rationale and justification for skipping my tithe, I heard God say, "You can't afford NOT to pay your tithes." I said, "What?" Not that I didn't hear Him clearly the first time, but I was shocked. He said it again, "You can't afford NOT to pay your tithes." After collecting myself, I was led to do the math. I lined up all the bills and decided I would only pay the minimum payments this time. If I paid the minimum and skipped my tithes, I knew I would have enough to get all of the bills paid. Wrong!!! I remember being two or three bills short. I did the math again and came up with the same results. I learned that if I kept my tithes, I still would not have enough money to pay all of the bills on time. Something would have to be late.

I said. "Okay God, you were right." I found out that using my tithe money would not allow all of my bills to be paid. I remembered the verse in the third chapter of Malachi where God gives us the challenge to do as He commands and prove Him to be the God who would pour us out a blessing that we would not have room to receive. In the past, I never needed God to prove Himself in my finances. I paid my tithes because it was what the bible required. This time, however, I was up for the challenge. I paid my tithes as usual and waited to see how God would work things out. And guess what? I paid my tithes and somehow every bill got paid on time. There were no bills left over to be paid that month. I cannot logically explain how it happened, but it did. Tithing is a spiritual principle that requires faith and trust in God and not in our incomes. I was truly amazed and extremely excited to share this wonderful experience with my husband.

God and I have never had to have this tithes conversation again. I tried God and saw His miraculous provision. It was amazing to see how I could pay all of my bills with ninety percent of my check when one hundred percent was not enough. Only God! I truly love how God puts us in our places and set us straight when we really think we are right in our attempts to explain to Him why we cannot do what He has told us to do. I just knew for sure that I was serving an understanding God who knew my heart and would not be bothered by me not paying my tithes for a short while. After all, I knew God was not broke. He could do without my little ten percent this time. I was right. God could do without it, but I couldn't. I needed to pay my tithes so that I could receive God's blessings. We must understand that when God asks us to do something or refrain from something, it is not to harm us but to help us. I will never forget this experience. After the initial shock of hearing: "You can't afford not to pay your tithes," I had to laugh and say, "Okay God, I get it!"

## How Did God Speak?

God spoke within the inner part of my spirit. I heard God clearly correct my thinking by telling me that I could not afford to not pay my tithes. He led me to write the bills out and I learned that keeping my tithes would not help me to pay every bill on time.

## God's Blessings or Satan's Gifts

I was managing a staff of about 60 individuals. One of those individual's job required that she make daily visits to my office. She was a young, single parent who worked hard to get ahead. She often talked about her aspirations to do more and achieve more in life. I would always take the time to listen and encourage her to go after her dreams. Many of our conversations would lead to the subject of church and the goodness of God. One day, she came right out and asked if I was a pastor, minister or something because she could tell that there was something different about me. I smiled and admitted that I was a minister. She smiled back and said, "I knew it."

As time went on, she began to confide in me about some personal things in her life. She confessed that she grew up in the church but had stopped going. She often talked about her desire to return to the church. However, she knew that she was still struggling with some things and therefore decided that she would return to church once she got herself together. I would often encourage her to return to the church before she got herself together because we cannot fix ourselves; we need God to do that. I told her that we should go to church with an intention and desire to do better and be better, but we have to trust God to help us get there. I told her that God is a forgiving God and He always welcomes us back with open arms.

Future conversations revealed that she had made a decision to return to the church. She was excited about renewing her fellowship with her church family. A couple of weeks later, she came in and began to tell me about how God had blessed her the previous week. After hearing about her blessing, I was sure that she was excited about the things she had received, but I was also sure that what she received was not from God. I cautiously informed her that we must be careful about the things we call God's blessings. Every good thing or perceived good thing does not always come from God. I informed her that the devil often uses the wrong people to bring good things into our lives. And although a thing might be good, we have to be careful about how we get it and why we got it. We discussed how God is all-powerful and quite capable of blessing us without resorting to any means contrary to His will or His word. She seemed to understand what I was saying.

She continued to go to church and started to serve in a ministry. She seemed to be very happy about serving in a ministry and before long she was serving in a leadership position like she had done before she left the church. She was busy doing the work of the Lord, but her lifestyle pretty much stayed the same. Later, she came in extremely excited about a big blessing she had received from a different person. She went on and on talking about her big blessing that she knew had come from God. She said that she knew it was from God because it was what she needed and it was so expensive. She wanted me to understand that it is not every day that a person would receive a gift such as the one she had just received. Again, I knew it was a wonderful gift, but it did not come from God. Once again, we talked about the ways God blesses His people. However, it seemingly went in one ear and out the next. Although she understood what I was saying about God blessing us as His followers, she still wanted to thank God for the gifts she had received and continued to receive for several weeks to come. She would come into my office smiling and grinning and say, "I know what you are going to say but let me tell you about my blessing." I just listened, shook my head and hoped that one day she would be able to tell the difference between God's blessings and the devil's gifts.

Later, I had a dream about this young woman. In the dream, God made it clear that He did not want credit for the things that Satan was bringing into her life. In fact, God was angry that His name was being associated with the gifts she received from these individuals. God does not stoop to the devil's level to bless His people. He does not bless us in ways that are contrary to His laws and statutes. I could not shake the dream because there was the feeling of impending death for this young woman. There was nothing in the dream that revealed death but the dream had an ominous feeling that she might die.

Surely, I wanted to dismiss this dream from my mind. I second guessed the dream and tried to rationalize and convince myself that the dream did not make sense because I could understand God not wanting credit for Satan's gifts, but I could not understand why there was a strong feeling of death. The more I tried to dismiss it and forget about it, the worse it got. There was a growing nervousness in the pit of my stomach that alerted me that this was no normal dream but a dream that had to be shared with this young woman. The thought of sharing this dream was making me nauseous. How was I going to do this? It was difficult enough to tell her that God was not pleased with her continued announcements of His blessings for things achieved in ungodly ways, but to tell her of this feeling of impending death was just too much for me to handle.

She walked in and out of my office twice the next day without me saying a word about the dream. Each time I saw her, the nervous feeling in the pit of my stomach got worse and worse, signaling me that this was something that had to be done. When she entered my office for the third time that day, I asked her to sit down and shut the door because I needed to talk to her. I gently and carefully told her that I had a dream that I did not want to tell her about, but I had to tell her. I told her both aspects of the dream; God's anger about being associated with ungodly gifts and an unexplained feeling that she could die.

I explained to her that these rare dreams that I have are like warnings. I explained that I believe that God gives these dreams to me to share with the individual so that they will have an opportunity to change their ways, seek God and pray. I explained that I believe if the individual change their ways then things might turn around and work out differently. Shockingly, she was not disturbed by the dream at all. She immediately began to tell me about a recent similar experience she had.

She told me that she had a strange feeling of death when a large flock of black birds landed on her front lawn. She said that she could not believe the number of black birds that continued to surround her house. She informed me that she associated this influx of birds with death. However, she believed that the flock of birds were a sign of her deceased father coming back to warn her or tell her something. She somehow surmised that her father was trying to tell her something good like how proud he was of her or something. Well, certainly this was not the reaction I expected but I was relieved. She basically corroborated the feeling of death in my dream. I encouraged her to please think about the dream and pray earnestly to God for answers and clarification about the dream as well as the flock of black birds that would not leave her front lawn. We hugged and she left my office as happy as she had been any other day.

The tension in my neck and shoulders left and my stomach returned to normal as I was telling her the dream. A couple days later she came into my office and said, "This is a pretty big position you have here in the agency, but I believe God has bigger things in store for you; bigger things outside of this job." She smiled and said, "I just wanted to tell you that." I smiled and said, "Thank you, I believe that you are right."

About 18 months later, I received a phone call at my new job. I had resigned from my State job as a Unit Administrator and was now serving as Program Director in the private sector. The caller wanted me to know the shocking news of the death of a former employee. She knew that I had worked with this young woman but she could not remember the young lady's name. She continued to describe her trying to jog my memory. Finally, it clicked and I called the individual's name and she said yes, that's the person. I was in shock and disbelief. "What happened? She was so young," I said. The caller informed me that she really did not know how she died because her family did not disclose a lot of information. I could not believe what I had just heard. I hung up the phone thinking to myself, she had so much life ahead of her. My heart ached as I thought of her children who she left behind. I sat for a while, shaking my head with tears in my eyes.

Just as I began to collect myself and get back to work, the dream that I had forgotten about flashed before my mind. I remembered the frightening dream that God prompted me to share with her. I remembered the sickness in my stomach, the fear in my heart, and the anxiety in my soul as I anticipated her response to the dream that I did not fully understand but knew that there was a strong feeling of her impending death. I remember asking her to sit down and shut the door because I had to tell her about the dream. Thinking about that day caused chills to run through my body. I was sad to hear of her passing, but I was relieved that I had the courage to do what God told me to do. A year and a half ago, I had to sincerely pray for God to give me the strength and the courage to do what He required. I was relieved that I was obedient and shared the dream that God had given me to warn her. I cannot imagine what I would have felt like if I had kept this dream to myself.

### How Did God Speak?

God spoke in a dream. This was not an ordinary dream. It was a dream that I could not forget; a dream that I could not shake. This was a dream that I tried to forget and discount because it did not fully make sense to me. I could understand God being angry and not wanting to receive credit for the devil's gifts, but I could not understand why it felt like she was going to die. I did not believe that one thing deserved the other or if one thing had anything to do with the other.

Because I could not make sense of the dream, I wanted to believe that it was something I should dismiss. However, the unnerving feeling in the pit of my stomach let me know that this was a dream that could not be ignored. I knew that this dream was a warning from God and He was holding me responsible for delivering His message. I believe that this dream was a warning because the dream did not show how, when, why or where the death would occur. It felt as if it was pending. I believe this warning dream was given to allow an opportunity for the young woman to make some changes in her lifestyle, which might have ultimately turned things around. This was no ordinary dream because it could not be dismissed, I could not rest and I had no peace until I shared the dream with this young lady.

### Got to Get Out of Here!!!

It was late one September evening; close to the end of the workday. I was sitting in my office feeling completely overwhelmed, frustrated, disgusted, burned-out, and downright TIRED! I was tired of multiple assignments and unrealistic demands from administration. Tired of the never ending meetings; working twelve to fourteen hour days and then going back to work on the weekends, just to keep my head above water. I was tired of working for an unsupportive and unsympathetic Administration which ignored middle management's attempt to advocate for their staff members; who were responsible for providing direct services to the city's most vulnerable families.

The large number of families that each worker was expected to service was a sure recipe for disaster as it was humanly impossible to provide excellent clinical services to such a vast number of individuals. It was becoming more and more difficult to work for an agency that refused to acknowledge the suggestions and recommendations of those who supervised and managed the front line staff. It opposed my leadership principles to be a part of an Administration which was insensitive and punitive to staff who were giving their all day in and day out. This on-going dilemma was a great source of stress, which caused me to be at a cross roads with regard to maintaining employment with this agency.

I have always taken my roles as Supervisor, Administrator, Manager and Director seriously. I believed that it was my duty to lead by example by demonstrating integrity, teaching with passion, encouraging with enthusiasm and holding my staff accountable with consequences. I have never been a fan of puppeteer leadership where one serves as a brainless puppet who dances to the puppeteer's music without thought, rhyme or reason. Once I believed that my leadership principles were being compromised, I knew I had a major decision to make.

In addition to the madness of the work environment, I was sick and tired of coming home late and missing dinners with my family. I was sick of having to answer my daughter's homework questions over the phone while I was still on the job. I was tired of hoping that my daughter would still be awake so that I could give her a big hug and kiss and talk to her about her day at school and anything else she wanted to talk about. I was hoping that she would still be awake although it was late and she should be in bed by then.

Ninety percent of the time she was still awake and I was so happy to see her come running to the door with a big smile on her face saying, "Mommy it's about time you got home!" I looked forward to reviewing and signing off on her home assignments even if my husband had already done so. This was our quality time together and I always told her that her hugs re-fueled me and gave me energy. They really did! And I think she enjoyed giving them to me as much as I enjoyed receiving them. I was thrilled to tuck her in at night and then finally be able to spend some time with my husband, who was my number one supporter and a great dad. I would not have been able to successfully work these long hours if he was not the loving and dedicated husband and father he was. He would patiently listen to me gripe, day after day, about the stressors of my workplace. I knew he had to be sick of hearing about it because I was sick of telling him about it, but I had to tell somebody.

So, after being sick and tired of being sick and tired, at the end of the day, I put the Do Not Disturb sign on my office door. This time I not only shut the door, but I locked the door as I knew that I was in no shape to receive any visiting staff; I literally had no more to give. I rested my head in the palms of my hands as I fought to hold back the tears. It felt like a ton of weight was sitting on my shoulders. I did not know what to do.

To make matters worse, someone who was careful not to knock on the door, decided to slide her requests under the door; a common practice, which further symbolized the never ending demands of the job. A locked door with a Do Not Disturb sign was no match for the steady stream of work, which prevented me from even the likelihood of a short reprieve. Shaking my head, I reluctantly walked over and picked up the work from the floor and returned to my desk. Then the phone rang. When I looked at the caller I.D I just wanted to scream! But I didn't; it was my supervisor who was housed in a different building. I answered the phone as calmly as I could; fighting harder to hold back the tears that silently began to make their way down my face. After asking questions and delegating more tasks, she asked what was wrong. I was too emotional to articulate all that was wrong so I just said that I was extremely tired.

She realized that something was deeply wrong because she always marveled at how I was able to remain calm in any situation. She often wondered how was it that I seemed to let nothing get to me or "ruffle my feathers" so to speak. She often asked how it was that I was able to handle the day-to-day crisis and workloads without becoming unglued. She wanted to know my secret. She was intrigued by my answer that I stayed in prayer and went to church. She would always say, "Still waters run deep" when she referred to my ability to handle problems, tasks, and people. This day however, I am sure that she realized that the still waters had somehow been disturbed.

Clearly, I was at the lowest point in my career as a Unit Administrator. I was responsible for supervising and managing supervisors and their staff and administrative support personnel, who were spread across three different buildings. I hung up the phone and said to myself, "I have got to get out of here. I am going to quit this job today!" Enough is enough; there was no other viable solution! In fact, I was so fed up that I decided that I would leave that night and never return again. Forget the two weeks' notice-- "I am out of here!!!"

Then reason and reality began to set in. I said, "Valerie, you have to give two weeks' notice; you must leave in a professional manner. Additionally, you must practice what you preach about doing things decently and in order." Then more reality began to set in as I thought about my financial obligations. Numerous questions began to flood my thoughts: How are you just going to up and quit when there are bills to pay? Who is going to pay your daughter's tuition for private school? Don't you know that you can't quit a job before you have another one lined up? Well, now that ton on my shoulders seemed to have gotten heavier and the tears turned into a steady stream. I could see no way out, but I could see no way to stay either. I really believed in my heart that I just could not stay on this job another day.

I said, "Lord you have got to help me and you have got to help me NOW! I am walking off this job and I am not coming back!" I did not want to leave in that manner but I had no other choice. I was physically and emotionally drained. At this point, the chips were going to have to fall where they may. I was willing to deal with the consequences of my decision. I sat there for a while asking God to please help me before I walk out.

Suddenly, I heard an audible voice that said, "Just get to December" I said, "WHAT?" I looked around my office and swiveled my chair around to see where the voice was coming from. Again it said, "Just get to December." I knew there was no one else in the locked office but me. I realized that this had to be the voice of God. Instantly, I had peace and the tears dried up. I smiled and said, "Yes, I can get to December." It was only three months away. There was freedom in knowing that there was light at the end of the tunnel and my departure had an official date.

Then, I begin to question the reality of quitting in December. I wondered what was so special about December or what was going to happen in December that was going to make it financially okay for me to quit. I could not figure it out; it made no sense to me, so I stopped trying to figure it out. I realized that I did not have to figure it out because God had spoken. I knew that if God said it, He would work out the details. All I needed to do was trust Him. I packed up my things and took my happy self home. I could hardly wait to tell my husband that I was quitting my job in December. I told him I could not explain what was going to take place in December, but I was sure that I had heard from God. I told him that I was going to trust God and see how He was going to work things out.

The next day I was so happy that my staff wondered what was going on with me. I could not stop smiling. I told them that I was looking forward to the Christmas holidays. I had so many ideas about how I was planning to decorate my house in a big way. I also explained that I was excited because I would not be coming back to work after Christmas. They looked with amazement as I told them about my experience in the office the day before. They were so happy for me, but they could not help but ask me several questions like: What did your husband say? How does he feel about the matter? Where was my next job? How long would I stay out from work? How was I going to handle things financially without having another job lined up? It was hard for anyone to believe that I was walking off my good state job without another job lined up. I smiled as I had no logical answers to most of their questions. I told them that I was trusting God.

I remember telling my friend and colleague, Wilma, that I can imagine how Abraham must have felt when God told him to move out from among his kinsmen and then He would show him the place he had prepared for him. Abraham had to trust God first and then start his journey on an unknown path. Later, God would show him where he wanted him to go. This was an exciting time for me. I heard God say, "Just get to December." I had to trust Him and plan my resignation for December. Then I would see how God would provide. I did not know what lied ahead but I knew I was going to be all right because I knew that God was in charge!

Everything fell smoothly into place. Several of the supervisors under my charge asked if I were absolutely sure that I was leaving in three months. I said yes. So they started looking for transfers to other departments in the agency as they were sure that they did not want to remain in this unit without me as their Unit Administrator. At least three of the seven supervisors were successful in getting their transfers within that three month time frame. God is good! They were happy for me and thankful that they had time to plan their moves as well.

I must say that God did provide. After December, I stayed off work for one year and there was no extra financial strain on my husband. I had accumulated so much Compensatory Leave, Personal Leave, and Annual Leave that I continued to receive a check for the entire time I was off. Although I was off, the checks kept coming and I kept accruing more time as I used the accumulated leave. It was amazing. I continued to be able to pay my bills, shop, dine out, and take vacations just as if I had never left the job. Clearly this was nobody but God!

### How Did God Speak?

God spoke in an auditory voice. I could hear the words spoken clearly in the atmosphere. It was so clear that I literally had to look around the room to be sure that no one had come through my locked office door. Hearing His clear and soothing voice immediately produced peace in my spirit. My burdens were lifted, my countenance changed from sad to glad and I had no doubt that I had heard the voice of God. Suddenly, I knew I could make it. I knew I could do what seemed humanly impossible just minutes before I heard His voice.

Before God spoke, I could not tolerate one more day on the job, but after He spoke, I eagerly came back to work in great anticipation of seeing how God was going to work things out. It truly was an exciting time as I continued to work, knowing that God orchestrated an end to my misery. I actually enjoyed my last three months of work as I anticipated and planned for my most festive Christmas ever!

### TFC Prayer
It was mid-day on a Saturday afternoon and I could not seem to shake the stress of my job. I was the Program

Director of a Therapeutic Foster Care Agency. For the most part, I liked my job. I really enjoyed working with my staff, the foster parents and the children. There was never a dull moment with regard to the day-to-day challenges that revolved around the families we served. Every day there was something new to tackle. Some things were predictable while other things caught us completely off guard. But whatever the day brought, we were up for the challenge. After all, solving problems, handling emergencies, improving communication, resolving conflicts, advocating for children and strengthening families are what social workers are equipped to do.

As the Director, I was tasked with dual responsibility; ensuring that the program was both clinically and fiscally sound and that it grew in the number of foster parents and children being served.

While it was my passion to ensure that the children's safety and well-being took precedence, I also understood my charge to grow the program by increasing the census number of children served, which ultimately dictated the financial security of the program. I eagerly accepted and met both the clinical and fiscal demands of the program. However, the more the census increased, the more the requests kept coming to continue to take it higher. Administration asked us to increase the numbers from 40 to 50, then 50 to 60, then 60 to 70, with no regard for the insurmountable work involved to achieve and maintain those numbers. My only reward for achieving a numbered goal was to receive a higher numbered goal.

It became evident that the TFC program was growing by leaps and bounds while other programs' numbers remained the same or decreased. It became clear that the TFC census was compensating for the low numbers in other programs. This pressure to increase the numbers became burdensome not only for me, but for the individuals who were responsible for completing the paperwork and intake demands that came along with children entering the program. There was a daily census log sent to all Senior Management to account for the final numbers in each program at the end of each day.

While my staff and I worked extremely hard to accomplish these numbers, we quickly learned that reaching the goals had become a never ending cycle; the more we gave them, the more they wanted. When would it ever end?

Now, you can understand why I was so stressed that Saturday afternoon. While I was cognizant of the fact that the program needed finances to run, I felt that we had met our financial goals year after year and now I believed that we were at a point where we should have been allowed to place our primary focus on strengthening children and families without the added pressure of the census. I was tired of hearing about numbers and I wanted to focus on the children and families.

Administration seemed to ignore the fact that every added number came with a name and a story. They seemed to have no regard for the children or their stories. I was so upset I felt like I could burst. I knew I needed to pray. So that is exactly what I did or tried to do that Saturday afternoon. While I was trying to pray, all I could think about was the ungrateful audacity of the administration to continue to ask for more children. So, I stopped praying and started over again and again. I was so frustrated and angry that I could not settle myself to pray.

I was so upset, that the only thing I could do was cry. I said, "Lord this is a shame. I am so upset with these people

that I cannot concentrate on what I am trying to pray about."
In fact, I did not know what to pray. My drive to succeed
coupled with their ever increasing demands for more was a
recipe for more stress and frustration. I do not remember
ever being in such a place where I was too angry to pray.
Therefore, I just gave up and continued to cry because I felt it
was a no win situation.

After a while, I heard the voice of God say to me,
"Don't worry about the census, pray for the children." "If
you pray for the children, then I will take care of the census."
This was amazing! I knew it was God because all of the
anger and frustration left immediately. I no longer felt the
pressure of increasing the number of children in the program.
God's requirement for the continued success of the program
was simple. All I had to do was to commit to praying daily
for every child in the program.

The Lord allowed me to know that many of these
therapeutic or emotionally disturbed foster children had come
from homes where nobody had ever prayed for them. Many
of these children did not have praying grandmothers or
mothers who covered them in prayer. Several of these
children had little to no contact with their biological mothers
or fathers and as a consequence, had never experienced a
positive, loving and nurturing relationship with caring
parents. God wanted these children to be blanketed with
prayer daily because despite their painful beginnings, they
were His children and they were very special and dear to His
heart. What a powerful revelation and an awesome and
honorable task I had been assigned from God. This was a
task that I welcomed wholeheartedly. Although I had often
prayed for the children, it was clear that this was a specific
and more intentional mandate. What was even more powerful
was that God gave me the specific things to pray for. I had to

get a pen and piece of paper and write down all the things God had spoken while on my knees.

The prayers were absolutely beautiful; it was comprehensive and orderly. The order was to pray first for the children, second for the foster parents and thirdly for the staff. All I could do was cry and write and cry and write. It was amazing to see how God could change my state of mind, lift my spirit, and provide me with a stress-free and easy solution to a problem that once seemed insurmountable. Only God could provide me with the answers I needed to continue being successful as the Director of this program without the added stress that came along with the job. This was a life changing prayer experience that lifted my burdens and the burdens of my staff, who worked closely with me to increase the census. Below is a list of the things that God instructed me to pray specifically for the children, foster parents, and staff under my charge.

## Prayer for Foster Children

- Pray for divine protection & safety.
- Pray that they will have positive/Godly friendships.
- Pray that the teachers, personnel, and administrators will see something beyond their exterior and go above and beyond what is expected to reach out to them and show them favor.
- Pray that they learn to forgive their parents so that they can open their hearts and minds to receive the love and nurturing being offered to them by genuine foster parents who really care about their well-beings
- Pray that they are protected from further abuse and neglect from perpetrators and future caregivers.
- Pray that they are protected from anyone who would misuse them sexually.

- Pray that they will learn how to bond and become an intricate part of their foster families.
- Pray for their ability to concentrate, to learn, and succeed academically.
- Pray that they will set positive goals for themselves and strive to achieve them.
- Pray for their salvation.

## Prayer for Foster Parents

- Pray that they will understand that the children placed in their homes are all unique and special to God.
- Pray that they will exercise wisdom and patience when rearing the children.
- Pray that they will genuinely love and care about the children in their care.
- Pray that they will be sympathetic and empathetic to the children's history.
- Pray that they will strive to understand the children's issues/diagnosis.
- Pray for their spiritual enlightenment and relationship with God so that they can provide the children with a spiritual foundation.
- Pray for their strength, energy, and emotional health.
- Pray for the overall health and success of their biological children.
- Pray for their ability to work with all members of the team in an effort to support the children.
- Pray for their salvation.

## Prayer for Social Workers

- Pray for their strength, energy and well-being.

- Pray for their relationships with their spouses or significant others.
- Pray for divine protection for them and their families.
- Pray for peace in their homes.
- Pray that they receive the help, support and encouragement they need from spouses or significant others.
- Pray that they have genuine concern for the children and families they serve.
- Pray that they will be sympathetic and empathetic to the children's history.
- Pray for their wisdom and ability to work collaboratively with members of the team.
- Pray for their willingness to go above and beyond to advocate for the needs of children.
- Pray for their spiritual growth and salvation.

What an awesome prayer experience to be able to hear God speak so clearly. I went from a place where I was too frustrated to get a prayer through, to a place of tears and total surrender, where I was forced to stand still and wait and listen for God to speak. Not only did God tell me what to do, but He gave me specific orders and guidelines as to how to get it done.

I know I do not have to tell you that the program continued to be highly successful. I prayed daily as God had instructed. I prayed in the specific manner and order He had laid out, and the census continued to grow. This time it grew without the added stress. I just sat back, prayed and watched God do just what He said He would do. I prayed and God took care of the census. In fact, before I left this program, the census had doubled and I cannot begin to tell you of the many success stories and achievements of the children who were a part of this program.

## How Did God Speak?

God spoke in a loving, caring, and gentle voice that I heard from the inner recesses of my spirit. This time it did not sound like the voice was outside of me but it came from within. It brought much peace, comfort and clarity. There was no doubt in my mind that God had spoken. He gave me the exact solution for growing and maintaining a successful Therapeutic Foster Care Program. However, God's solution was easy and it produced no worries, stress, anger, or frustration.

The very next day, on Sunday morning, my pastor, Bishop Walter Scott Thomas Sr., preached a message that seemed as if he overheard my prayer experience the day before. Although I cannot remember the specific text or title of his sermon, I do remember the point that he drove home like never before. He preached about God putting His people in leadership positions for the expressed purpose of doing His will. He talked about promotions coming from God and not from man. He wanted us to know that our success in these God ordained leadership positions would come about because of God and God alone. He told us that we will not be successful because of our good looks, connections, education and degrees, but we will be successful leaders because of the power of the Holy Spirit which will lead, guide and direct us in our efforts. WOW!!! This was confirmation through the man of God, my pastor, the Shepherd of the house of God, where I am a member.

God spoke to me first through prayer. I heard His calm, steady voice from the inner being of my spirit. He spoke again the next day through the man of God who preached a word that confirmed everything He had spoken the day before. If I had any doubts that I had heard from God

Saturday afternoon, (of course I did not), I would have known for sure that it was God based on the word preached on Sunday morning.

### Make the Call Now!

I had been gone from state services for about 12 years. I was working in the private sector. Several of my older friends who were still working in State service were now looking forward to retirement. They were talking about pensions and social security. Although I was nowhere near retirement, it was time to start thinking about it more seriously. I realized that the state offered retirement benefits that the private sector did not offer. So I made up my mind that I would return to state service and add to my former years of service.

One day, I received a work related call from a former colleague in the private sector who had retired and now was working for the state. We chatted for a while and then I told him that I was interested in returning to state service. He informed me of a job that he thought I might be interested in. He provided me with the name and number of an employee who worked in personnel. I hung up the phone and called the number, but the individual's voice message indicated that she was on leave. I decided to call back later. Several weeks passed but I forgot to call back. When I finally remembered to call back, I decided against it because I figured that the job I was interested in had probably already been filled by now. Occasionally, I would come across the person's name and number on the top of one of my many legal pads, but I somehow continued to put the call off.

One Monday morning while I was busy at work, my eyes glanced across the information on the top of the legal pad just as it had many times before. This time, however, I heard a voice that said, "Call now." This clear and authoritative voice came while I was diligently working on a project; I had no intention of making the call. However, this directive could not be ignored. I stopped right in the middle of what I was doing and made the call. I inquired about the position and was told that particular job was no longer available but was informed of a different supervisory position. I was asked by the lady who answered the phone to fax required information for the available position. She seemed excited about my call and informed me that she remembered me and would fast track my information to the appropriate department. She made me aware that I was calling at the perfect time as the pay scale for this particular position had recently been increased. Of course, I was excited to hear this news! I went home for lunch, gathered the information, returned to work and faxed the information to her the same day.

Later that afternoon, I received a call from my supervisor informing me that she and other managers were being called into an emergency meeting at 3:00 p.m. and she wanted to meet with me afterwards. Around 4:15 p.m., we met as scheduled, where I was informed that due to a financial decision made by upper management, I was being laid off from the agency. She wanted me to know that this decision had no reflection on my job performance and it was a decision that had to be made. The decision impacted all programs across the board. She apologized for the short notice as this decision was out of her control. The executive team decided they could no longer afford the salaries of temporary staff in leadership positions. Therefore, all temporary supervisor assignments ended that Friday.

While my supervisor thought this was bad news, I smiled and told her that I was completely okay with the news. After all, she and I already had several candid conversations regarding my desire to return to the state. With that being the case, I knew that the assignment would eventually come to an end.

With this happening, I could hardly wait to tell her about the experience I had earlier in the day. I informed her that I had already spoken with someone at the state's personnel office after I was urgently prompted by God to do so. I told her I had already faxed over my resume and application for a supervisory position within the state. I was so excited to testify about the goodness of God, who somehow has a way of preparing us for the unexpected even when we do not know what the unexpected is. Since my supervisor and I are both Christians, we were able to talk about the awesomeness of God, who always provides for His people. She thought she was delivering bad news that would cause me to be upset and come to tears. Instead, she saw someone that was at peace with the agency's decision. I reassured her that I would be all right. We ended the meeting with hugs and a plan for how I would end my week. Only God could allow us to end a meeting with this kind of news on such a positive note.

On Wednesday, two days later, I received a call asking me to come in for an interview on Wednesday of the following week. I was told that if the interview went well, there was a good chance that I would be offered the job by the end of next week. Needless to say, I interviewed and was offered the position. Who can beat the timing of God? Who can give you the specific directions to securing your future? Who knew that one job would end on Friday and I would be offered a better paying job, with better benefits, the next Friday? Only God! I can truly say that it literally pays to hear God when He speaks!

## How Did God Speak?

God spoke from the inner parts of my being. His voice could not be ignored as it was very authoritative; immediately grabbing my attention. It seemed to come out of the blue; nothing I was doing or thinking at the time prompted it. There was something about this directive that let me know that the timing was now. I knew that I had to stop what I was doing and do what God was prompting me to do. Although I did not know why I had to move right away in that moment, I moved. And a few hours later, everything made sense. Once again, God was showing me that He is my source. He is my provider. He knew that my current job was about to end in a couple of days and another one, with my name on it, was waiting for me but I had to make the call. Oh yeah, remember the job that I really wanted that was already taken by the time I made the call? Well, after serving in a supervisory position for a year, the other job became available again. I interviewed and yes, the job that I originally wanted is now mine. God is good and favor isn't fair!

# Chapter 6 - Scriptures

1. But my God shall supply all your need according to his riches in glory by Christ Jesus. *Philippians 4:19 KJV*

2. Take delight in the LORD, and he will give you the desires of your heart. *Psalm 37: 4 NIV*

3. When the righteous thrive, the people rejoice; when the wicked rule, the people groan. *Proverbs 29:2 NIV*

4. The LORD had said to Abram, "Go from your country, your people and your father's household to the land I will show you. *Genesis 12:1 NIV*

5. For promotion cometh neither from the east, nor from the west, nor from the south. But God is the judge: he putteth down one, and setteth up another. *Psalm 75:6-7 KJV*

# Chapter 7
## *What If ...*

# Chapter 7
## *What if ...*

Recently, I learned that there is a branch of history called counterfactual history. This is when a theorist attempts to determine how our world might have turned out differently if certain historical events had not taken place. For example, what if slavery never existed? What if fathers were never ripped away from their wives and children and sold like cattle to the highest bidder? And if slavery had never happened, how might the mentality or psychology of those enslaved be different? What if the color of one's skin had no effect on how an individual is perceived, treated, or afforded opportunities? Counterfactual theorists ask the question, "What if?" as it relates to history. But I ask the question, "What if?" as it relates to our spiritual ability or inability to hear God's voice. I wonder how the peaks and valleys of our individual lives might differ as a result.

When I started writing this book, I had no knowledge of counterfactual history, but I have often pondered the "what if" questions as it relates to one's spirituality and one's belief about God. What if God really is speaking all of the time but we are missing His messages? And if we cannot hear, how does that shape our spiritual perception of God?

Man has often been perplexed about tragedies and natural disasters that take the lives of innocent people. It is during these times when men really doubt or question the authenticity of a loving God. It is during these difficult times that we hear the resurfacing questions such as: If there is a God, then why this and why that? If God really loves us, then why would He allow this or that? Clearly these are questions none of us can answer because we are not God. We are incapable of explaining or trying to make sense of things we cannot comprehend; especially when these things appear to be in direct opposition to what we believe to be the character and nature of God. When we encounter these incomprehensible things in life, it is not our duty to try to defend God because He needs no defending…..He is God! This is precisely the time when we must trust Him.

Although I am convinced that we will never have all the answers to why some things happen to us and our world, I still cannot help but wonder if God might be speaking and warning us about some natural disasters and the horrific misdeeds of men. I continue to believe that God loves us so much that He often warns, directs, and redirects our paths so that we can avoid many dangerous situations. However, I believe that we often miss the messages because we are not tuned in to the spirit that speaks.

I remember many years ago when I was just a youngster in the church, there was a visiting prophetic preacher by the name of Evangelist Walker who was able to warn us of various things that were about to take place in our world. He was even able to tell us about future changing weather patterns. He was able to foretell the exact times of upcoming storms. He was able to predict inflation down to the month and year of its occurrence; predicting the rising cost of certain food items. The predicted price of a loaf of bread seemed unbelievable at the time because the predicted price was so much higher than the current price. It made folks wonder how they would be able to feed their families if these prices became a reality. Well, time passed, the prices went up and God continued to provide for His people.

This preacher had a certain peculiarity. It was obvious that he spent quality time in the presence of God. He walked, talked, and prayed with a special kind of anointing. His countenance reflected a deeper knowledge and wisdom of the things of God. Evangelist Walker's commitment and dedication to seeking the face of God caused him to stand out from other preachers. He knew things that only God could reveal. However, if you were to look at his small to medium frame you would see that there was nothing extraordinary about him physically. In fact, he may have been a little on the thinner side due to his diet which included regularly scheduled days of fasting. In the grand scheme of things, we realize that he really was no different than you and I. What separated him was his desire to be in God's presence and his desire to hear what God was saying. The word of God declares that God does not favor one man over another and He draws close to those who draw close to Him. With that said, it is clear that we too can be privy to some of the things that only God knows, if we spend the appropriate quality time in His presence.

The scripture tells us that we have been made out of the image of God. He has made us a little lower than the angels. And when God created the world, He gave man dominion over the animals. All of these scriptures help us to understand that God loves us and values us more than the creatures of the earth and the fouls of the air. Yet, the scripture lets us know that God still provides for the sparrows. Every day God directs the sparrows to places where they find the exact portions of food they need to sustain them for the day. It is no coincidence that the birds are not dying from starvation. I believe that these birds are attuned to their creator who helps them to successfully navigate their environment in an effort to get their daily needs met. These birds and other animals not only rely on their creator for food, but they often rely on Him for their safety.

Many scientists confirm this notion because several studies have shown that some animals can sense major changes in the weather. For example, worms are known to flee rising groundwater. Birds are known to be sensitive to air pressure changes. They often hunker down before a big storm. Researcher, Von Mergenthaler, believes that animals can pick up the "infrasonic" sound pulse created by storms and earthquakes and get a head start on fleeing to safety. Many animals are known to run inland, fleeing from the shoreline. Other animals travel to the woods where they are safest during a storm. Researchers in Florida have found that sharks flee to deeper waters before a big storm or hurricane. They also may be sensing the risks and water pressure changes. Scientist, Michelle Heupel, states that animals may be more attuned to their environment than we give them credit for. While they may not understand what is happening, when things change, it triggers some instinct to move to an area that is safer for them.

I cannot help but believe that if God is loving enough, sensitive enough, passionate enough, and concerned enough to equip worms, birds, cattle, sharks and other animals with an innate ability to sense danger, then how much more did he equip us? Again, scientists realize that these animals may not understand what is happening but they are able to sense the changes in their environment and move to safer grounds or waters. I believe that the key to these animals successfully avoiding danger is their ability to sense and move. Unlike us, they do not have the capacity to intellectualize, rationalize and reason, so they rely on their internal instinct to move.

My brothers and sisters, we too must learn how to trust the spirit within us and MOVE. There comes a time when we must not lean on our own understanding but we must acknowledge God who directs our paths. We must grasp the fact that our ability to move is based on our ability to trust God. It is a wonderful thing to know that we have been created higher than the animals. It is awesome to be able to function intellectually, develop elaborate plans, make concise decisions, and arrive at well thought out conclusions. However, there comes a time when we must put our intellect aside and rely on the spirit within. We must trust our creator, God, because much of our success, our safety and our ability to reach our goals are a direct correlation to our ability to hear and our willingness to obey God's voice.

Can you hear the words spoken in written scriptures? Have you ever had a Rhema word experience while reading the word of God? Can you hear the voice of God through the pastor/preacher, teacher, parent and other persons of authority? Can you hear the message in the God-given dreams and visions? Can you hear the message in the signs and songs all around you? Can you hear from the inner and outer parts of your being; your spirit? Can you hear? We must realize that the ability to hear God's voice is a very personal and serious matter.

And if you can hear, are you able to move and obey even when it doesn't make sense on your human intellectual level? Be mindful of the fact that it is God who is speaking, so there is a great possibility that it might not make sense to you. His ways and His thoughts are far from ours. God is speaking from a perspective of infinity and eternity. We, on the other hand, only have knowledge of and access to limited information in our past and present. We cannot speak with certainty about anything concerning our future. Therefore, if we want to be privy to the things that God is willing to share with us, then we must avail ourselves to those practices that sharpen our ability to hear. If we are going to successfully climb mountains, jump hurdles, and avoid many of life's pitfalls, then we must be able to hear God, trust God and move! If we do not trust God, then we will not move.

Let's review my personal testimonials discussed in chapter six. What we will find is that in most cases, if not all, there was always some element of fear, some element of the unknown; some inability to fully make sense of or comprehend what or why God was saying or directing me to do a certain thing. Oftentimes, there was an element of timing or a sense of urgency. However, despite all of the unknowns and uncertainties, there was always a time within those experiences when I could sense that it was God who was speaking. There was something different about what I was hearing because it came from my inner spirit with clarity, conviction and authority. In every experience, I could hear God's voice clearly. There was never any doubt about the clarity of what I heard. I knew what I heard, I could repeat what I heard, and I remember exactly where I was and what I was doing when I heard it. However, there were times when I questioned and/or could not clearly understand the meaning of what I heard. During those times, I continued to pray to God; specifically asking Him for a greater understanding or revelation of what He was saying. There were other times when I heard God clearly and everything made sense. The message was crystal clear.

On the other hand, there were times when the message was clear, it made sense to me and I understood the command or directive but I wanted to know the how, when, where and/or why. Sometimes God provided those answers and in other instances, the answer was not provided. If I did not receive the answers to my additional questions, I quickly realized that those answers were not necessary at the time. It was those times that I totally trusted God and waited for Him to work out the details. My job in those situations was to hold on to what I heard, wait with great excitement and anticipation for God to bring His word to pass.

I have found that when we are consistent and intentional about our communication with God; when we have a praying spirit, we will have no trouble determining when God is speaking. When we know that it is God who has spoken, we must trust, obey and move in faith so that we will achieve God's desired outcomes for our lives and the lives of others. I am convinced that if we are not able to hear God's voice, then we are not living our best lives.

I often reflect on the many times I have heard God's voice. I am still amazed at some of the things I have heard and seen as a result of God speaking to me in dreams and visions. As I reflect on these times, it is evident that I heard His voice and moved in faith; oftentimes, with fear and uncertainty, and watched God do some amazing things. However, I have often wondered how things might have turned out if I were not able to hear God's voice during those crucial and/or significant times. Hence, the purpose for this chapter entitled, What If? Let's look deeper into these testimonials to determine how things might have turned out if I were unable to hear God's voice.

## Praying for Nana
## What if…

What if I did not have a prayer life? What if I had not gone to church that Friday night? What if I had never seen the vision of my grandmother's death while praying for her?

What if I had not prayed for God's mercy to hold back the hand of death to allow me time to speak to and witness to my grandmother about her salvation?

If I had not seen this vision, my family would have been totally blind-sided by her death because she was not ill. In fact, she appeared to be a picture of good health. When we saw her last, she was happy and content as always. The thought of losing her was the farthest thing from any of our minds. When I saw the vision of her in a coffin, I was shocked. I could not believe what I was seeing. I pleaded with God to allow my grandmother more time so that I could talk to her about accepting Him as her personal Savior. After praying and pleading for some time, I saw my grandmother sitting up in a chair smiling. I immediately knew that God had answered my prayer. God added time to her life so that I could talk with her about being saved. If I would not have had this vision, my grandmother might have died without Christ and therefore, would have had to spend eternity without God.

While it is not uncommon to lose a loved one unexpectedly, the important thing about hearing God's voice through this vision was having the opportunity to share the vision with my grandmother and offering her the prayer of salvation which led to her acceptance of Christ as her personal Savior. The other thing that this vision did for me was confirm that God really does hear and answers prayers because He answered the prayer of an eighth grader.

It also confirmed for me that He loved me greatly because he cared enough to spare my grandmother's life, at my request. I saw God literally extend His mercy when He moved her from a dead state; stretched out in the coffin, to a living state; sitting up in the chair smiling. This happened right before my eyes. It is one thing to hear the preacher say that God answers prayers, but it is another thing to learn this truth for oneself at such an early age.

I had this vision late in the month of October. My grandmother died early in the month of January the following year. She passed away about two and a half months after that vision. We were still shocked and devastated by her passing. We later remembered and discussed the vision I had prior to her death. This did not help with the pain, sorrow and grief that came after her passing. It was pretty hard especially for my mother and my father, who loved her like his own mother. For me however, the vision seemed more real. The actual funeral was sad, but it felt like Déjà Vu. Emotionally, I had already witnessed my grandmother's funeral. I had already seen her body stretched out at the front of the church and I had already cried most of my tears. The peaceful thing about being present at her actual funeral was I knew she was safe in the arms of God and one day we would see her again.

**The Car of My Dreams**
**What If…**

What if I had not prayed about this car on that Friday evening before I went to sleep? What if I had never had the dream which revealed that we would find the car at the Nationwide Dealership on Eastern Avenue? What if God had not confirmed in my dream that I would find the car and be able to identify it by the small insignificant cigarette burn in the driver's seat?

If I had not heard the voice of God concerning this car in my dream, I would not have been able to convince my dad to return to this dealership a second time. If I had not had this dream, I would have given up on getting that particular car. However, in the grand scheme of things, it really would not have been that big of a deal. I merely would have had to decide on a different color four-door Sentra or I would have had to choose another model red car. Either way, I would have still gotten a new car that week.

Having God speak to me through a dream regarding this car was not a necessity. Purchasing this car was not a life-changing event. Clearly, my life would not have changed or been significantly impacted if I did not get this particular car. This car was merely transportation; my own transportation which I was proud to have, but it still was just a car.

The significance of this dream for me was the realization that God cares about the little things in life that concerns us. We often believe that we should only pray about major things in life. We believe that God could care less about our desires; especially our desire to purchase a particular color car. In fact, most of us believe that God is too busy addressing real issues to be concerned about the little things that matter to us. Most of us believe that God would not take the time to speak to us about the location of a red car with a cigarette hole in the driver's seat. Interestingly enough, He did and I learned early in life that I could pray about anything. I learned that God has the capacity to handle the big and little concerns of life. He cares enough to speak to us about anything that we commit to Him in prayer. The bible clearly informs us that God will take care of our needs but this dream allowed me to know that God sometimes gives us exactly what we want!

**Keeping me Safe from Unseen Danger**
**What if...**

What if I could not hear God's voice within the innermost part of my being? What if I had refused to call my fiancé because the directive did not make sense? What if I had decided to trust my gut instead of the spirit? What if I had continued to walk with the crowd which provided me with a false sense of safety? What if I could not hear God's voice the first time, the second time or the third time?

If I was unable to hear God's voice that night, I am convinced that I would have been raped and possibly murdered. I am so grateful to God that I was able to hear His voice. As I was leaving the library, I heard God clearly direct me to call my fiancé to pick me up at the library and drive me to my car. I could not understand why this was necessary so I hesitated and tried to dismiss this directive several times. I could not fathom why I should ask my fiancé to drive 45-50 minutes to the library only to drive me five minutes to the parking lot across the street. I felt safe and I was happy to be driving home in my new red four-door Nissan Sentra I had just purchased over the weekend.

However, after hearing the command so forcefully the third time, I knew that it was something that I had to do. I realized at that point that I needed to be obedient whether it made sense or not. I took the risk of sounding like a fool and made the call just as God had commanded. Fortunately, my fiancé was understanding and did not hesitate to come and pick me up. (God already knew that he would not hesitate to pick me up).

Once we got to my car and saw the intended rapist, in a stooping position on the driver's side of my car, jump up and run off into the woods, we knew why I had to make the call. It was then, that everything made sense. There were no other cars on the bottom lot. The rapist expected me to be alone where he was ready to attack. He was kneeling below the car, out of sight, where I would not have seen him until I walked around to put the key in the door. If that had been the case, it would have been too late for me. The rapist would have figured out that it was the prime time and opportunity to carry out his plans, but I am glad to report that God's plan for me prevailed.

Once again, God shielded and protected me from unforeseen harm and danger. I am alive and well to tell this happy ending to this story because I was able to hear and obey the voice of God. I heard a directive that did not make sense but I trusted God enough to do what He said. My ability to hear and my willingness to obey saved my life from the rapist who intended to do me great harm…. But God!!!

## The Storm
## What If…

What if I had not committed to pray the day of the storm? What if I had not decided that I would pray all the way home until I made it safely to my front door? What if I was unaware of the potential dangers of the storm? What if God had not caused me to be focused on what seemed like the biggest, strongest, and sturdiest tree on the block of already fallen trees? What if I could not hear God's voice shout MOVE as I approached the tree I thought would never fall?

If I had not heard the voice of God within the innermost part of my being, I truly believe that I would have been seriously injured or possibly a fatality from that storm. I believe with all of my heart that I would have been smashed in my car by the humongous tree that was featured on the 6:00 p.m. news that evening. The tree was so enormous that it covered the entire street and literally stopped traffic from moving in both directions. I was the last car to pass the tree before it fell.

After speeding to the opposite lane, I was able to see and hear the tree fall in my rear view mirror. I passed this tree within seconds of it falling. It was almost like an outer body experience because things happened so quickly. I heard God's voice shout MOVE!!! I moved swiftly, pushing my foot on the gas pedal and gripping the steering wheel to maneuver my car away from the tree that I thought was unmovable. I moved just in the nick of time.

I was aware that the weather was bad before I left college. I had waited a short while hoping the storm would subside before leaving. I then decided to take my chances. However, I knew I did not want to take my chances without prayer. I knew that the storm was dangerous and I needed God's protection. I made a conscious decision to pray from the time I got into my car to the time I arrived safely at my front door. Today, I am a living witness that God does answer prayers. He protected me in the storm and guided me safely to my front door. I am alive and well today to let the world know that prayer works. I made it home safely because God spoke and I heard His command to move!

## Prophecy – A Spiritual Gift
## What If …

What if I had not taken the time to seek God for my spiritual gift? What if I had not set time aside to seek God in prayer; asking Him to clarify the gift I felt but could not articulate? What if I had not taken the bible with me in that prayer experience; asking God to speak to me through His word?

If I had not taken the time to pray and ask God to speak to me and show me my spiritual gift in His word, I would still be wondering what gift I was given. If God had not made this gift crystal clear in prayer and through His word, I would still be running away from the gift instead of embracing the gift.

Once I shared this experience with my former pastor, the late Bishop Fred Page Sr., he explained the prophetic gift and informed me that the prophet is the mouthpiece of God. He immediately assigned me to work with the other women in ministry despite my hesitation to move forward. He smiled and informed me that he had been watching me for years and he was patiently waiting for me to acknowledge the gift he already knew existed in me.

God showed me my gift in His word. I then understood my charge and the penalty for not speaking the word that God gives me to warn, encourage, or edify the body of Christ. God also confirmed this gift through two women of God and my pastor who sensed this call of God on my life years before I did. This was an unforgettable prayer experience which revealed the gift that I could no longer ignore and no longer deny.

## God Knows My Heart
## What If...

What if I had not purposed in my heart to skip paying my tithes for a short while? What if I had not taken the time to talk to God about my decision; providing Him with what I thought was good justification for skipping at the time? What if I did not hear Him speak clearly in my spirit, "You can't afford NOT to pay your tithes?"

If I had not heard the voice of God that evening, I would not have witnessed the supernatural provision of God. I had always paid tithes and never had any problem giving back to God the tenth that He required. I believed fully in the principle of tithing and had been a willing participant in the tithing process since childhood. I had consistently experienced the blessings of God and had seen Him open doors and make ways for me and my family. I had seen His provision first hand and never questioned or doubted the benefits of tithing.

Up until this time, I had never been in a place where I thought I could not afford to pay tithes. I always paid my tithes and always had enough money left over to do what I needed and wanted to do; therefore tithing was never an issue for me. However, as a young, married couple with a two person household income that had been reduced as a result of a temporary layoff, I thought for the first time that I was now in a position where I could not afford to pay tithes; at least for the time being.

I am so grateful for this experience because for the first time I had to do what the scripture challenges us to do… pay our tithes, try God and see what He will do. In the past, I paid tithes because I was taught to do so and as a result I had always experienced His favor and blessings. However, at this juncture in my life, I thought it made sense to stop temporarily and resume when my husband was back to work.

If I had not heard God say, "You can't afford NOT to pay tithes" I would not have been prompted to find out why I couldn't afford NOT to pay my tithes. I would not have taken the time to do the math which proved that keeping my tithes still would not have allowed me to get every bill paid. This was the first time in my tithes paying experience when I really had to trust God. If I had not trusted God to do what He said He would do, then I would have never witnessed God's miraculous provision. I paid my tithes and watched God help me to pay all of my bills with ninety percent of my check when the math proved that one hundred percent of my check was not enough.

Until that time my testimony about tithing was limited. I could testify that God would meet our needs if we paid tithes because my needs were always met. I had never been in a position where I had to decide between tithes and a bill. I could not relate to those who said, "I would pay tithes but I cannot afford to." I always believed that we should pay our tithes because God said so and if He said so, then we could do it despite our financial situations. Somehow I always knew that it was an act of faith and obedience. The reality is…my spirit knew what my life experiences had never taught me. Thus, I could tell others about this biblical principal from a spiritual perspective but not from an experiential perspective.

This experience, however, allowed me to witness, first-hand, what I believed all along but this time I had a personal testimony to back up what I believed. Now I was able to give others an example of God's miraculous provision and challenge them to try tithing for themselves. For the first time, I was able to relate to those who wanted to pay tithes but believed they could not afford to. This experience provided me with the proof that if we give God His ten percent, He will work everything out. I know He will work it out because He did it for me. I was now a living witness that God could make ninety percent go further than a hundred percent. So, if you have never tried this principle, I want to encourage you to take God's challenge. God's word challenges us to try Him and see if He won't open a window and pour us out blessings that we do not have room to receive. Like me, I am sure that there are countless others who can testify to the fact of needing more room; more closet room, more shoe room, more cupboard room, more jewelry room, etc. because the rooms that we have are all full and running over because God does what he says. He pours out blessings that we do not have room enough to receive.

## God's Blessings or Satan's Gifts
## What If…

What if I had not been praying for my coworker? What if I had not been witnessing to her on a regular basis? What if I did not have the God-given dream which had a foreshadowing of her death? What if I did not have the courage to share the dream with her?

If I had not been witnessing to my coworker and praying for her, I probably would not have had the dream. The dream confirmed the things we had often discussed in my office. God was clear that He did not want credit for the things that Satan was bringing into her life. Although I did not see her in a dead state, there was a strong feeling of death over her life.

This was a dream that I could not shake. I knew that I had to share it with her although I could not fully understand it. I could not understand why death was associated with her calling Satan's gifts God's blessings, or if one thing had anything to do with the other. In my mind, this infraction surely did not deserve death but I was sure that death was looming over her.

If God had not given me this dream, then I would not have been able to warn her. I would not have been able to encourage her to pray and ask God for clarity and mercy. If I had not had the courage to share this dream with her, then her blood would have been on my hands. In other words, God would have charged me with her death had I not delivered His word of warning. Several months after leaving the job, I received the news of her passing and I was truly saddened.

After collecting myself, I remembered the dream. I remembered the conversation we had in my office about the dream and I was so relieved that I had done what God told me to do.

## Got to Get Out of Here!!!
## What If...

What if I had not prayed prior to walking off the job? What if I had not asked God to speak now so I would not have to leave without a proper resignation? What if I did not know that I needed a RIGHT NOW word from God? What if I had not taken the time to pray before doing something stupid? What if I had not heard God say, "Just get to December?"

If I had not prayed before I left the office that day, I would have left and never returned. I was at the end of my rope with this job. I truly believed that I could not take one more day. The stress and the long hours had become overwhelming and I was unwilling to return another day. At that juncture, I was willing to accept the consequences of leaving without a proper resignation because I was just that tired. I do not know if I would have come to my senses after I had gotten home that night, but in the moment, I was done. My back was against the wall. I knew it did not make sense to leave and never return but I was in no mood for rationale...I wanted out!!! I knew I needed direction from God. So I asked God for His help because I was burned-out and depleted; I had no more to give. I asked God to speak and He did just that. I heard God say, "Just get to December." The voice was so audibly crisp and clear that I had to look around to see where it was coming from. I knew that I had heard from God because immediately, I felt the burden lift from my shoulders and I witnessed the tears disappear from my face and my mood changed from sad to happy in a matter of seconds. I felt an extreme sense of peace.

It was the month of September and I knew I only had to work for three more months. I knew I could come back to work tomorrow because there was light at the end of the tunnel. I did not know what was so special about the month of December. I did not know how I would be able to take care of my financial obligations, but I was not concerned. I had a feeling that everything would be all right. I was now excited to come to work the next day because I knew that I had been released to leave this job in three months.

I could now use the remainder of my time to end properly and prepare my staff for my departure. I could hardly wait to share the good news. Everyone was shocked to hear that I was leaving without another job lined up but they could see that I had peace of mind and joy in my heart. The peace and the joy became contagious as so many were happy for me and baffled at the same time. They had so many questions that I could not answer. I could only tell them that I had heard from God and everything was going to be all right, although I could not tell them how it was going to be all right. I knew that I had clearly heard the voice of God and now I was waiting and trusting God to work out the details.

God literally ordered my steps and directed my path as to how and when to submit my Leave of Absence paperwork and when it was all said and done, I was able to take a year off from work and still receive a pay check every two weeks because of the many hours of compensatory time and accumulated annual leave that I had earned. This was a time when I truly witnessed the provision of God up close and personal. I was able to use this time off to get closer to God. It was such a joy to be able to routinely read and study the word of God without interruption or time constraints. It was also a time when I was able to focus on family, healthy eating and routine physical exercise. During this time, I was able to improve in the areas of mind, body and soul. This was truly a time of spiritual, emotional, intellectual, and physical growth, renewal and rejuvenation. My ability to hear God's voice made it possible for me to take a year off from work and become more holistically empowered without the added stress of any financial struggle or strain.

**TFC prayer**
**What If…**

What if I had not attempted to pray about the ongoing demands of the job? What if I did not know to confess to God that I was too angry to get a prayer through despite my desire to pray? What if I didn't know that sometimes we just have to wait and meditate on God when we lack the words to say? What if I had never heard God's plan for how to manage the program from a spiritual perspective? What if I had not heard God speak the beautiful daily prayer that He wanted me to pray for the children, foster parents and staff?

If I had not taken the time to pray or attempt to pray, I would have never heard the Win-Win plan of success for the TFC program, that I was responsible for managing. God made it clear that I no longer needed to be stressed about the administration's continued need to increase the census. He told me that if I prayed, He would take care of the census. I could hear God speak the words of the prayer verbatim. The prayer was loving and beautiful; the only thing I could do was listen and cry. These tears were tears of relief, joy, peace, and amazement.

God charged me with the responsibility of praying for His children who had been placed in the foster care system. God's plan for success was easy and stress free. God's plan was clear and specific. Although I had often prayed for the children, the words God had given me were specifically tailor made for the children in this program. This prayer covered every aspect of these children's lives. It was an amazing prayer and an awesome experience. I can still remember the soothing feeling of warmth coupled with a gentle and loving voice that sounded like music in my ears.

The frustration and anger about an unappreciative administration, which only seemed to be interested in financial gain was gone. I was now able to walk into the same office with the same people asking for the same things but not be bothered by them because I had the Win-Win plan and solution for the real success of the program. The Administration would get what they WANTED but most importantly, the children, parents and staff would get what they NEEDED; the blessings and the covering of the Lord. Once again my peace was transferred to my staff that also felt the effects of the census saga. They were glad to know that I had heard from God and received an easy solution to what was once an on-going frustrating dilemma. Many of them joined me in daily prayer for the children, foster parents and staff of this TFC program. We could calmly sit back and watch the census grow and the children succeed. We prayed and God did the work!

**Make the Call Now!!!**
**What If...**

What if I could not decipher the voice of God? What if I could not hear His voice in the midst of work demands and assignments? What if I could not hear the authority in God's voice which directed me to "Make the Call now!!!"

It was a good morning. I was energetically working to get the things done that needed to be completed for the day. I had already had my caramel flavored Keurig cup of coffee and was moving right along with no problems. The morning was busy but productive. In the midst of completing my work, I heard the voice of God which said, "Call Now!!!" I knew immediately what call to make. I knew God was urging me to make the call to the individual in the state's personnel office. I sensed that the timing was right. I stopped what I was doing and immediately began to look for the name and number of the person written at the top of one of my legal pads.

I found the pad, made the call and everything went like clockwork. The person I spoke with remembered me from years before. She was very helpful and extremely excited to hear from me. She was eager to let me know that I was calling at the right time because the salary for the position which I was applying had just been significantly increased. She encouraged me to get my paperwork in right away as she would ensure that it got to the right people. I completed the application and gathered the supporting documents as requested and the rest is history.

I am once again employed by the state of Maryland and I am currently serving in the position I initially inquired about which was not available at the time. I am back in state services in a great position, making a decent salary with benefits because I heard God's voice twice with regard to my employment with the state. The first time I heard God's voice, I was so frustrated with my job that I was ready to walk away from my state job without a proper resignation (I had no intention of ever returning) but I prayed first and asked God for direction where He told me to, "Get to December." The second time, I was in the private sector desiring to get back to the state when I heard God say, "Make the Call Now!!!" I made the call and was offered a state job one week later.

Hearing God's voice the first time allowed me to leave state services properly so that twelve years later, I could successfully re-enter state services because I left in good standing. Only God knew that one day I would want to return. When I left the first time, I said I was never coming back. I am grateful that I have lived long enough to fully understand the saying, "Never say Never."

## Chapter 7 Scriptures

1. So God created mankind in his own image, in the image of God he created them; male and female he created them. *Genesis 1:27 NIV*

2. What is mankind that you are mindful of them, human beings that you care for them? You have made them a little lower than the angels and crowned them with glory and honor. You made them rulers over the works of your hands; you put everything under their feet. *Psalm 8: 4-6 NIV*

3. Look at the birds of the air; they do not sow or reap or store away in barns, and yet your heavenly Father feeds them. Are you not much more valuable than they? *Matthew 6:26 NIV*

4. Be careful for nothing; but in everything by prayer and supplication with thanksgiving let your requests be made known unto God. *Philippians 4:6 KJV*

5. Will a mere mortal rob God? Yet you rob me. "But you ask, 'How are we robbing you?' "In tithes and offerings. *Malachi 3:8 NIV*

# Chapter 8
## *Let's Go Deeper*

# Chapter 8
## *Let's Go Deeper*

### Introspection
### Keeping It Real

As I look deeper into the Cook Library Incident, (Keeping me Safe from Unseen Danger), I realize that this incident is the most personal for me. If I were unable to hear God speak during this time, this incident would have left me the most traumatized. If I had not heard God speak that night, I would have been affected physically, psychologically, emotionally, socially and spiritually. If Satan's plan had been executed, I would have been raped. Rape has the power to attack the mind, body and soul; leaving one with feelings of hopelessness, guilt and shame. It is a brutal and calculated act that affects a person's total being. Therefore, I have chosen to look deeper into this experience in an effort to emphasize the importance of being able to hear God's voice.

This incident will also allow me to show how we might charge God falsely if we are not able to hear Him speak. If we are unable to hear and heed God's warnings and directions, then we will accuse Him of not loving us, not stepping in to rescue or save us from horrific and sometimes deadly situations. I cannot emphasize how important it is for us to hear God's voice. We will never have a clue of the things we are missing out on if we are not in tuned with His voice. If we do not know how to recognize God's voice, we will have to endure unnecessary heartache and misfortune. If we are unable to hear God's voice, we have no one to blame but ourselves.

I have worked many years in the Human Services field and have found it astonishing the number of times I have heard individuals blame others and make excuses for their own ineptness, failures, and poor choices. Many people find it easier to blame others for their problems. Many people blame their parents, spouses, churches, communities and even the system for their issues. While all of these individuals or entities might play a major role in the life and development of individuals, it is important that at some point we learn to let some things go; move forward and make a decision to do what is necessary to change the trajectory of our own lives. The task of helping individuals, acknowledge, take ownership and responsibility for their own lives require much skill. The goal is to help individuals understand that taking responsibility for oneself requires a certain level of effort, maturity, focus and discipline. Too often we decide that it's just easier to point the finger at others rather than do a self-examination and change the things that we have the power to change.

Unfortunately and even sadder, there are many times when we blame God for our problems. We blame God for things that we have brought upon ourselves. We blame God when we must deal with the repercussions of our own poor choices and decisions; many times we have not followed God's instructions, which were clearly laid out in His word. We also blame God for things that we could have avoided, but we do not know that we could have avoided these pitfalls because we did not hear God speak to direct us otherwise. Please understand what I am saying here. I said, WE did not HEAR God speak. The point I am trying to make is… we were not in position to hear. We were not committed to reading His word and communing with Him daily through prayer. As a result of our disconnection with God, we did not hear what we needed to hear; we missed out on the specific word that He spoke to us regarding our immediate need. God did speak to help us financially. He did speak to help us physically. He did speak to help us guard our hearts and minds. He did speak to ensure a hedge of protection around us, but we could not hear Him. Think about it my friends, there is no way we will ever know what God said if we did not hear Him say it!

One of the greatest teachers of Gospel Ministry and Sermon Preparation, Reverend Darius A. Smith, always taught his students (Ministers in Training) the importance of being transparent–the ability to be honest and allow our authentic self to be illuminated in the word that God has given us to deliver. When preachers can constructively disclose truth in their sermons, it allows those in the pews to relate and identify with them and their humanity.

Transparency helps others to understand that preachers often endure pain, heartaches, disappointments and insecurities like everyone else. It helps others to understand that preachers are imperfect and are sometimes faced with fears, doubts, anxieties and overwhelming concerns just like those they are preaching to. When the preacher receives a word from God, the word should be applied to their individual lives first; they are never exempt from the word that they bring. Have you ever heard the preacher say, "I am preaching to myself and if you don't say amen, I will?" Authenticity helps others to know that the preacher too must be faithful and steadfast in prayer if they are to weather their own storms and get through the trials and tribulations they face in their daily lives.

So, in that vein, it is my desire to be completely transparent about how I would have felt if I had not heard God speak the night of the Cook Library incident. As I reflect on that night, the first thing I know to be true is IF I had not heard and obeyed the voice of God, I would have been raped and possibly murdered. The second thing I know to be true is IF I had not heard God speak and somehow lived through this ordeal, I personally would have had some REAL PROBLEMS WITH GOD; the God I loved, served, trusted, worshipped, adored, and strived to please. (Please understand that it is possible for us to love God and have a form of godliness and still neglect to do the things that help us hear God's voice).

I would have had problems with God because I know Him to be omniscient, omnipotent, and omnipresent. If I had not heard Him speak that night, I would have accused Him of being omniscient, (all knowing) yet acting as if He was unaware of the rapist's intentions. I would have accused Him of being omnipotent, (all powerful) yet exercising no power to stop the rapist from committing this ungodly act and lastly, I would have accused Him of being omnipresent, (being everywhere at the same time) yet not present with me in a time when I needed Him most. If this act had occurred, I would have felt abandoned by God and I would have falsely accused Him of failing to exercise His authority in any of the three areas. In my mind, I would have believed that He did nothing to keep me safe or protect me from harm.

The Social Worker in me shudders to think how my life might have been altered? My experience as a Mental Health Therapist makes me wonder what DSM diagnosis I might have received. Additional probing clinical questions that come to mind are questions like how might my self-esteem, self-concept, confidence, and ability to trust and form healthy positive relationships been affected? How might my personality have changed? Would I have become timid, fearful and withdrawn? Would I have become angry, insensitive, and bitter? Would I have become wild and promiscuous? Would I have developed a fear or a hate of men? Would I have decided to involve myself in relationships with women because I felt safe and understood that they could not harm me in the same manner of the male rapist? Would I have still gotten married? And if so, would the marriage ever be right? Would I have suffered from Depression and/or Post Traumatic Stress Syndrome? What if? Why, why and why again. The list of questions could have gone on and on, but the root or foundational meaning of all of these questions points to one piercing question which is…. did God really love me?

Does God love us? This is a thought-provoking and poignant question that many folks ponder when they are confronted with horrific personal situations and devastating global disasters in the world. We cannot help but wonder if God loves us when we must suffer and endure the debilitating effects of sicknesses and diseases that attack our bodies. Sicknesses that seemingly sneak up on us out of nowhere and send our lives into a tailspin that leaves us gasping for breath; wondering, "How did this happen to us or our loved ones?" We question God's love for us when we are faced with betrayal and discrimination. We wonder how long we must endure these setbacks and injustices. How long God? We ask over and over again.

We wonder about the love of God when we must defend ourselves against lies, character attacks and false accusations of the smiling faces that cleverly attempt to orchestrate our demise. We question the love of God when we learn that family members and so called friends are secretly jealous and subtly envious as they sit back and quietly manipulate situations in an effort to discourage our hopes and kill our dreams. We wonder about God's love when we continue to love, support, and encourage individuals who seemingly lack the ability or willingness to reciprocate. We wonder about God's love when we have to helplessly stand by and watch the ones we love slip from time to eternity. We watch quietly with tears streaming down our faces, outstretched arms, and broken hearts wishing we could somehow stop the inevitable. We hope and pray that God would mysteriously turn back the hands of time. It is during these times when we wonder if God really knows or understands our pain.

These heart-wrenching and emotional situations often cause us to feel alone and abandoned by God. We often wonder if God really sees what is going on. Sometimes we wonder what we have done wrong to deserve this or that. Oftentimes, we come to the realization that we have done nothing to deserve what we are going through just as others who have experienced the same things have done nothing to deserve what they have experienced. I have come to realize that much of what we endure is just life and life happens to all of us. The important key to living life is to not live it without Christ.

We have come to accept and understand that certain behaviors and lifestyles might dictate or predict certain negative outcomes. However, it is difficult to comprehend why certain outcomes befall individuals who have lived an otherwise clean and upstanding life. In other words, why do bad things happen to good people? Sometimes things do not correctly add up according to our calculations. When this happens, we are often left feeling numb, bewildered, and disappointed. We cannot help but wonder where God is in these difficult and unfair situations.

Sometimes the appearance of God's absence might cause us to question our doctrinal teachings and our faith in God. We begin to wonder if God really is the God we read, preach and teach about. Sometimes the devastation of traumatic events cause individuals to walk away and turn their backs on God because the belief is that God could have and should have done something to turn certain life events around. I honestly believe if I had not heard God's voice that night I would have questioned my beliefs.

You see, I really believed in the power of God. I really believed that he loved me, cared for me and protected me from seen and unseen dangers. In fact, I believed that I was the apple of His eyes and I sensed His favor upon my life from an early age. Thus, to have experience an ordeal as horrific as rape would have shaken the foundational core of all I believed about a loving God. I would not have been able to figure out why a loving God/Father would not have done something to protect His child.

Amazingly enough, I have come to realize that when we think God is doing nothing He really is doing something. He is speaking. He is leading. He is guiding. He is protecting. He is orchestrating. He is warning. He is directing and re-directing us all the time. Unfortunately, however, we often miss His signals, are unable to sense His promptings and are hard of hearing. (Please slow down and re-read these few sentences again). I really want everyone to know that God is speaking and He is intricately involved in our day-to-day lives. Sadly enough however, we will never know how involved He is if we cannot hear Him speak.

The fact of the matter is, we don't know what we don't know and we don't know what we didn't hear. For example, God may have said, "Do not accept this job," but you accepted the job because you could not hear God. After accepting the job you found the job to be so demanding and time consuming that it eventually cost you your marriage and family, which subsequently led to a nervous breakdown and hospitalization.

In this case, there is no way you could have known the repercussions of taking this job, neither would you have known that God had spoken to warn you against taking the job if you could not hear God's voice. This is a clear example of not knowing what you didn't know and not knowing what you didn't hear. I am convinced that we miss out on so many blessings and we endure so many hardships because we are not hearing the voice of God. God wants us to succeed. God wants the best for us. It is God's desire that we avoid many of the unpredictable pitfalls in life, but we will continue to miss out and suffer unnecessarily if we are not in position to hear God speak.

If our ears are clogged up, if we are not paying attention, if we are not praying, if we are not reading God's word, if we are not taking the instructions of our biological and/or spiritual parents or parental figures, if we are not receiving the word of God from God fearing men and women who have been called to preach the gospel of Jesus Christ, if we are not attuned to the spirit, if we are not finding the time to sit, meditate, and be quiet, then we will not be able to hear God. It really is that simple. We must do something to get something from God. Please understand that knowing what to do but not putting it into practice will not help us. If we do what we know is right to do, then God, who is faithful, will fulfill His promises every time.

Thankfully, I heard God's voice the night I was leaving Cook Library. If I had not heard Him, I must confess that, I, like countless others, would have erroneously concluded that God did not love me. I would have arrived at this conclusion in error because God did speak. In fact, He spoke several times; each time more forceful than the previous time. Once again, however, if I could not hear God speak, I would have never known He spoke, nor would I have realized how much He loved me and how consistent and persistent He was in His efforts to keep me safe.

I cannot begin to imagine what it must feel like to be God, watching His children continuously make a mess of their lives because they are missing or ignoring His messages. And then to add insult to injury, we turn around and accuse Him of not loving us. How could He not love us when He sacrificed the life of His only begotten son to ensure our salvation and our healing? Why wouldn't He want to commune with us daily to ensure that we might obtain the abundant life that His son's death secured for us?

I don't know how you feel about it, but I want every blessing that God has for me. I am striving to live in a place of unshakable faith and trust in God; a place that brings inner peace in the midst of chaotic and unsettling situations. I am glad that I have personally experienced the unexplainable peace that comes along with hearing God speak. I can now look back over my life and appreciate the times when I have been down, had my back up against the wall, and suffered the hurt, betrayal and lies of men. I am grateful for those experiences when I did not know who or where to turn but I knew I had the privilege of prayer. I always knew that I could cry out to God; tell him all about my troubles and wait for Him to speak!

Now, let me stop right here just to be clear that although God speaks, He does not always protect us or shield us from every unpleasant situation. If He did, there would be no room for our spiritual growth and development. If we never went through anything in life, then our witness about God's goodness would be limited. We would not be able to talk about the God who CAN and WILL with confidence, conviction and authority. We would never have a testimony about God's power and faithfulness if we never needed Him to be powerful and faithful in our personal situations. How many of us know that nobody can tell our story like we can tell it? We must strive to do everything in our power to commune with God so we can hear His voice clearly. If we could consistently hear God's voice with distinct acuity and precision, we would undoubtedly know that He loves and cares for us unconditionally and we would never have reason to doubt this basic foundational truth.

Our finite minds attempt to plan for our future with great anticipation and limited predictability. We prepare for what we hope the future will bring, knowing full well that the next second is not promised to us. But when God speaks in the now, He speaks knowing what our future holds. These could be things we would never imagine, both good and bad. When God tells us or shows us these things, it is not for us to try to figure out why He is saying what He is saying. It is our responsibility to know His voice and respond with obedience.

We must understand that it is not God's fault if we cannot hear Him. He has made it possible for us to hear. We can hear through His word, through pastors, a song, dreams and visions. We can hear through our parents and those in authority. We can sometimes hear a pronounced, distinct auditory voice or a quiet subtle small voice in the innermost parts of our spirits. But are we listening? Are our lines of communication open? Are we obedient? Or, have we allowed sin to separate us from God and from discerning His voice?

There are sins of commission- the wrongful acts/deeds that we commit that are contrary to the word and will of God, and there are sins of omission- the acts/deeds that we fail to practice and adhere to, which separates us from God. Sins of commission and sins of omission are both equally detrimental to our ability to hear the voice of God.

We can readily accept the fact that lying, stealing, fornication, and adultery, separate us from God but we underestimate how our lack of reading and studying God's word, our lack of prayer and fasting, as well as our lack of praise and worship, all seriously mutes the voice of God in our lives. I firmly believe that if we work on the sins of omission, the sins of commission will take care of themselves. I do not believe that an individual can earnestly study the word of God, seek His face through prayer and fasting and then willfully commit sin on a consistent basis. When we commit to practicing the things we should do then we have less difficulty refraining from the things we should not do. When we spend time with God, He makes us better. When we commit to the things of God, our spirits become stronger than our flesh and when the flesh and spirit goes to war, the spirit will win. The key is staying connected!

Isn't it frustrating when you are in a deep conversation with a friend on the cell phone and suddenly realize that there is silence on the other end? Maybe someone touched the mute button by mistake, or maybe the call failed due to a poor reception area or a dead zone. Whatever the case may have been, communication has been interrupted. So it is with God. Sometimes we are going through the motion, but there is silence on the other end. Let's not make those mistakes that cut us off from God and mute our hearing. Let us not travel too far from His presence that our prayers will drop and our communications fail. If we find for some reason we have become disconnected to God, then we should simply do what we are accustomed to doing when we talk to our friends on the phone. We should push the redial button, find out what happened and start the communication all over again; picking up where we left off.

We can push the redial button in our communication with God by re-committing. Recommitting to the practices that bring us closer to God; the things that will keep our communication lines flushed so that God's voice can come through. We must commit to the things that will not only allow us to hear His voice but obey His voice because what good would it do us to hear but not trust Him enough to obey. We must (unequivocally) undoubtedly believe that God knows and wants what is best for us. Therefore, if He tells us to do something, go somewhere, write something down, call, visit, pray or help someone, then we should do just that. God only asks us to do the things that He knows we are capable of doing. When we obey God, He blesses us and others. After all, we are helpers one to another. God uses people to be a blessing to people. Often times, God has answered our prayers but He cannot get our blessings to us because His people are unable to hear or unwilling to trust and obey His directives. When our hearing becomes dull, we hinder God's blessings for ourselves and others.

Please know that these blessings that God is trying to get to us and others are not always material things. Sometimes all we need is a word from the Lord; a word that has the power to change our lives and situations. Sometimes we just need to go where God leads us so that we will be in the right place at the right time to connect with the right person at the opportune time and season of our lives. Sometimes we need to respond to the urging of God to reach out to others by calling, encouraging, or forgiving someone so that they are released to be all that God has called them to be.

When we increase in the things we should be doing, we realize that God really does love us and it becomes easier to trust and obey Him. It becomes easier for us to let go of our will for His will because we know and understand that His will is always better than ours. This unbreakable connection with God allows us to hear and obey His voice despite all that goes on around us. What we learn in this relationship with God is that our obedience to God blesses us beyond measure and it elevates us to new heights. Obedience strengthens, establishes, and encourages our hearts because every time we obey God, somebody is blessed. When we are able to witness these blessings, it helps us to trust God even more. We realize that our obedience to God is always for our own good and the good of others. Hearing and obeying work hand-in-hand and produce the outcomes that God desires for us.

In conclusion, I close with the title of this book, When God speaks, Can you hear Him? It is my utmost prayer and my earnest desire that we will not miss out on what God is saying. I pray that every hand that touches this book and every eye that daunt these pages will be prompted by the Holy spirit to do what is necessary to hear God speak.

### "Take Aways"

There are some very significant points I would like for every reader to take with them after reading this book. These are what I call, "Take Aways." These are the things that are important to remember as we become more intentional about hearing God speak to us.

**Take Away #1 – Prayer is the Key.**

Much of the voice of God is derived out of prayer. In most of my experiences, God spoke as a direct result of prayer. Having a praying spirit allows God to drop clues and nuggets of wisdom into our hearts and minds. Having an open heart and mind, in the prayer process, allows God to freely give answers, directives, confirmations and strategies for overcoming the obstacles that we encounter in our daily lives. This is essential in winning battles and conquering the attacks of the enemy.

By having a consistent prayer life, God is able to grab our attentions in the midst of all that is going on around us. It's during our prayer times that He will speak to us about our concerns. He may whisper something in our ears, show us the motives, intentions and deceptions of those around us, and He will also warn us of things to come.

Remember, as His children, God will speak to us about any and everything that matters to us. Prayer is the key to having a successful life. He is waiting patiently for us to come to Him in prayer. It is up to us to know when He is speaking and then obey after hearing His voice. Make it a habit and incorporate prayer in your life. You will be amazed and blown away after witnessing God move in your life!

**Take Away #2 – God Speaks to His children at every age, stage and season of their lives.**

God will speak to us at different ages, stages, and seasons of our lives. It does not matter if we are a budding flower in the early stages of life or a perennial flower that has weathered several seasons of our lives. Our race, gender, position, or socio-economic status does not matter either; God will always speak to His children.

The examples below prove that God will speak to us at every age, stage and seasons of our lives:

- It was when I was just a youth in middle school that I received the vision of my grandmother's death.

- I was a young adult in college when I had the dream of the car dealership that had the specific car I wanted to purchase.

- While I was in college, God guided me safely through a storm by MOVING me out of harm's way.

- In college, I had the foreboding dreams of a possible rape and later heard the instructions from God to avoid the rapist.

- I was a young adult, with an infant child, when God spoke to me about my gift and calling.

- I was in a management position when I heard God's instructions for when and how I should resign from my position without having another job lined up.

These events show how consistent and faithful God is. He will never leave or forsake Us. He will definitely speak to us (his children) at every stage of our lives.

**Take Away #3 – Dreams and Visions from God might require additional prayer in order to understand what God is showing us.**

There will be times when God will speak through a dream or vision. Sometimes we may not initially comprehend the meaning of what we see. There is a familiar saying, "A picture is worth a thousand words." While this saying may have some merit, we cannot use our own logic or make assumptions about what God is showing us. I have found that dreams and visions require further prayer and meditation before they can be interpreted correctly. These are times when we must remain in God's presence and consult Him for clarity and understanding of what He wants us to know.

Sometimes when God shows us a vision, the picture we see may not make sense. For example, one time I was earnestly praying and interceding on behalf of an individual. While I was praying, I saw a picture of a large hand. I tried to shake it off because I could not understand or believe what I was seeing. Later, I began praying for this individual again and once again I saw this large hand. Now, I realized that the hand I saw the first time had some significance. I began to ask God to reveal to me what He wanted me to know about this Hand as it related to this individual. I continued to pray for this person when I heard God's warning for this individual.

God wanted me to inform this individual of two things:

(1) He loved him. He had him in the palm of His hand and NOTHING could pluck him out of His hand.

(2) This individual needed to repent (turn from the things he was doing) or else he would suffer greatly. . .

In this scenario, I had to seek and pray to God more in an effort to understand the vision of the large hand that I saw while I was praying for this individual.

Clearly, I would not have gotten this warning message or understood the purpose of the hand had I not sought God further. There is no way I could have come to this understanding by merely seeing the picture of the hand during prayer. Only God could have revealed the meaning of this image. When God gives us an explanation of a dream or vision, it will literally leave us shocked and amazed. It is an awesome experience to receive such a detailed revelation of what God has shown us. Not only does it bring about clarity but it also enhances our relationships with God. As mentioned in previous chapters, He continues to speak to us through visions and dreams.


**Take Away #4 – God often speaks futuristically.**

We serve an all-knowing God. He knows the beginning from the end and He knows the individual plan that He has for each and every one of us. I believe that God loves us so much and is so excited about our future that sometimes it is difficult for Him to keep it to Himself. Therefore, He shows us snippets of what is to come. Sometimes, He whispers in our ears the truth about who we REALLY are. He places drives, instincts, and certain proclivities within us that gently move us towards our destinies.

Although God often speaks to us about our future, He is careful not to give us too much too quickly. He often provides us with a snapshot of our future because He knows we would be too overwhelmed by the entire album. I believe that God's plans to bless, prosper and promote His children are so vast that He can only share bits and pieces with us at a time.

God will often allow us to see ourselves in an unfamiliar place. This place is ALWAYS bigger than where we presently are. Seeing this place can be both exciting and scary. The excitement of what God shows us can cause us to run faster, while fear, on the other hand, can cause us to slow down.

Oftentimes, we fear that we are not ready; we fear that this move will drastically impact our lives and the lives of those closest to us. We sometimes believe that God is moving too fast. The truth of the matter is…we may not be ready at that moment, but God knows when we will be ready. This is a time when we must be patient, trust Him and wait for His plan to unfold.

Sometimes when God shows us our future, we begin to doubt God or question how this could be, as our current situations do not line up with what we see, hear, or feel in our spirits. We sometimes become perplexed because we cannot envision the final outcome. We often want to know the how and when but God often remains silent on the matter; providing minimal information on the process of our becoming who He has destined us to be. This is a process that we must remain steadfast and endure until the appointed time.

We must understand the importance of holding on to what God has told us or shown us. We must meditate on it and keep it fresh in our hearts because the enemy is quick to make us doubt what we have heard or seen. He is quick to make us think that it is too late for it to come to pass. We cannot allow the devil to make us feel unworthy of the future plans that God has for our lives. But KNOW that the devil is a liar and if God said it then it will come to pass.

I will never forget a dream I had where I was preaching in a huge and unfamiliar setting. I sat amongst preachers I did not recognize. The big semi-circle podium on the pulpit was unlike any I had ever seen. In the dream, I stood and began to approach the podium when I heard God say, "Take off your shoes because the ground that you are standing on is Holy Ground." I took off my shoes, stepped up into the oddly shaped semi-circled podium and began to preach the word of God with much power and anointing. This dream was so real; I shared it with my father and other church members. I was desperately trying to figure out where this place might be. After some time, I gave up. I realized that this was a place that I had never been,

During the time, I was a member of Highway Church of Christ, under the leadership of the late Bishop Fred Page Sr. I grew up in this church and was a very active member. I gained my spiritual foundation there; however, I could feel a tugging in my spirit that was leading me to more.

As time went on, I began to think about other Apostolic Churches that I might be interested in joining. The idea of joining any denomination other than Apostolic was never a thought in my mind. After all, Apostolic was all I knew and of course we had our own preconceived notions, ideas and misconceptions about other denominations just as I am sure other denominations had or have about the Apostolic Church.

At any rate, my daughter, Courtney, who was an Elementary student at the New Psalmist Christian School, was very excited about the New Psalmist Baptist Church that was being built on the grounds of her school. She couldn't wait to visit the church once it was built. One day she came home shouting, "Mommy, mommy, we really have to visit the new church now because I helped to build it!" She explained that every student got a chance to lay a brick on the ground. I finally agreed to visit this beautiful edifice that had been built right before our eyes.

Upon our arrival to the church, we were greeted and welcomed by many smiling faces. The service was phenomenal; spirit-filled, structured, timely and accented with a powerful word from an awesome pastor by the name of Walter Scott Thomas Sr.

Courtney and I enjoyed visiting this new church. For the next couple of months we would visit New Psalmist and then return home to attend our home church with my husband. One Sunday, my husband decided to see what all of the excitement was about. He decided to visit the new church with us. Like us, he thoroughly enjoyed the service. My family continued this routine of attending both churches for several more weeks.

One Sunday my husband grabbed my hand and said, "Let's join." As he was rising from his seat, I gently pulled him back to remind him that this was a Baptist Church. While I loved visiting this church, I could never join because we were Apostolic (Holiness). I told him that I was worried about what the saints would say. They would think that I had lost my mind. He smiled and said he was not concerned and we joined the New Psalmist Church that Sunday.

A few weeks later, while attending an afternoon service, I watched as pastor Thomas reached out his hand to assist an older female minister to the podium so that she could speak about breast cancer awareness. I watched as his hand gently guided her to step up into the semi-circle podium. Instantly, the dream flashed before my eyes! My mouth dropped and my eyes widened as I looked around the sanctuary in awe of what I was seeing.

### "This is the Place!!!"

"This is the place I saw in my dreams! That is the oddly shaped semi-circle podium  that I had to step up into to preach," I explained to my husband.  I looked around the church and realized that this was the place in my dreams; the place I had never been. I was filled with emotions because  at that very moment, I realized that I was exactly where God wanted me to be.

Every aspect and detail of the dream was true. The entire architectural layout of the church was exactly as I saw it. From the oddly shaped podium in the pulpit to the way the pews were situated on the main floor and the balcony. It was amazing watching the dream unfold right before my very eyes. Imagine dreaming about a church months before it was actually built.

This is a prime example of what I mean about God speaking futuristically. No wonder I could not figure out where this place was and despite the vivid detailed description I provided to others, they could not figure this place out either. No one could figure out where this place was because at the time of my dream, this place did not exist. However, God knew that it was coming and He knew that I would get there.

Oddly enough, by the time the dream flashed before my eyes, I had already been in the church several times. I had visited for months and had been a member for a couple weeks but had never recalled the dream until then. I believe that God's timing is impeccable. He does not allow anything to happen before it is time. I believe that God did not allow me to remember the dream until after I had joined the church because He wanted me to undoubtedly know that it was His will that I had joined this Baptist church which He had already confirmed was Holy Ground. The only thing I could say was, "Wow!"

After reflecting on the vivid reality of this dream, a nervous feeling came over me. Because every detail of this dream was so exact, I could not help but wonder about myself being in the pulpit. I thought to myself, "Will I actually preach in this church one day?" My heart skipped a beat as I quickly dismissed the thought. "No way," I thought to myself. It would be virtually impossible for me to ever preach in this big church.

Besides, I was quite comfortable being the new member on the pew. I was quite content coming to a church where few people knew my name. I had no desire to be known or overly involved. In fact, I quite enjoyed the opportunity to finally be able to blend in with the crowd.

Well, how many people know that our plans are not always the plans that God has for us? This dream was futuristic in many respects. Not only did I step out of my comfort zone to join the New Psalmist Baptist Church, but I also preached my "New Psalmist Initial Sermon" in that big church. By the time of my initial sermon, the podium had changed, but I already knew that I was standing on holy ground!

This dream also confirmed a word I heard God speak years prior. He said that, "He was about to tear down the denominational walls that separated His people." I heard that word and I believed that word, but I never thought that I would literally be a part of this significant move of God.

**Take Away #5 – God helps us to stay one step ahead of the enemy.**

When we remain committed to God and His principles, He will provide us with plans, strategies, and directives that will help us stay one step ahead of the enemy. As we commit ourselves to God, we will find that He is even more committed to us by the things He does for us. There are times when God will show us the plans and motives of our enemies and provide us with a strategy to throw them off course or beat them at their own games. When we obey, by implementing God's instructions, it often takes the enemy by surprise. It is during these times when we smile because we have the inside scoop; we know things that others do not know. It is like having the test questions, in advance, to the final exam.

Our all-knowing (omniscient) God knows the tricks and plans of our enemies. By having a relationship with Him, He gives us advanced notice (a heads-up) to any attacks from the enemy. God prepares us for what lies ahead. He is committed to seeing us succeed in all areas of our lives. Get to know Him. It is an awesome feeling to know that we can walk and talk with a God who has all the answers.

**Take away #6 – We must learn how to turn off the noise.**

Noise is all around us—in our environment and our heads. It is distracting; diverting our attention away from the practices that sharpen our hearing and promote spiritual discipline. Noise forces us to simultaneously give our attention to multiple issues and concerns, leaving little time for the pertinent things that God has laid at our charge. We must be wise enough to understand that this noise is not always negative or destructive. It can be positive and productive, yet it is noise just the same. Noise prevents us from putting God first; it cuts into our quality time with God.

Noise is: busyness, distractions, hurriedness, confusion, unrest, jitteriness, being scattered; exactly where the enemy wants us to be. If he can move us away from our connection with God, he is victorious.

In spite of life's demands, we must be relentless in keeping out the NOISE. It is imperative that we find a place of tranquility to keep out the noise. It is in this space where we will more clearly hear the voice of God.

A couple of things that can be done to get to this place are turning off the television and walking around our homes with a prayer, song, or scripture in our hearts. We must invoke a spirit of praise and worship in our homes. This will create a shift in the atmosphere so that we can enter into God's presence. It's best to have a room or special area in our homes where we can spend quality time with God. This is often referred to as our prayer room or our secret closets. We must tune out or block the noise! I encourage everyone to find at least two or three places in their homes where they can intentionally go to feel God's presence, hear His voice, and meditate on His word and goodness.

**Take away # 7 – God is speaking all the time and He is always eager to commune with us.**

God has been speaking to His people since the beginning of time and He is still speaking today. He desires to have an intimate relationship with His children; a relationship where He is able to effortlessly commune with us throughout our daily lives. The ability to hear God is our responsibility. It is up to us to get in the hearing position and stay there. We must remain connected to God. Don't miss out on all He has in store for your life!

## Chapter 8 Scriptures

1. Above all else, guard your heart, for everything you do flows from it. *Proverbs 4:23 NIV*

2. Keep your lives free from the love of money and be content with what you have, because God has said, "Never will I leave you; never will I forsake you. *Hebrews 13:5 NIV*

3. For the LORD shall be thy confidence, and shall keep thy foot from being taken. *Proverbs 3:26 KJV*

4. So do not fear, for I am with you; do not be dismayed, for I am your God. I will strengthen you and help you; I will uphold you with my righteous right hand. *Isaiah 41:10 NIV*

5. For God so loved the world, that he gave his only begotten Son, that whosoever believeth in him should not perish, but have everlasting life. *John 3:16 NIV*

# My Prayer for You!

Father, God I pray that you would bless every reader. I pray that you would give each person a hunger and a thirst to seek your face and to hear what you are saying. Father, I ask that you would help us to understand the importance of spending quality time with you. Help us to slow down and not become overwhelmed with life because we have not learned how to put you first. We say and believe that God, is first in our lives but our actions do not line up with what we say. Help us to seriously evaluate the time we are spending with you. Help us to make the necessary adjustments. Help us to become intentional about our time with you because no time can compare to the time we spend in your presence. Help us to whole-heartedly come into your presence; cause us to be fully present in mind, body and spirit. Open our ears that we might hear and our hearts that we might fully receive all that you have for us. We recognize that you have the power to make things happen-- heal sick bodies, lift heavy burdens, fix what's broken and restore everything that has been torn down. God, I pray that we will not miss what you are saying. I pray that we will not ignore what you are saying. I pray that we will not doubt what you are saying, and I pray that we never forget what you have said. Help us to hold on, cherish, and value the words you have spoken to us and help us to wait patiently for you to bring every word to pass. Lastly, I pray not only for the ability to hear but the willingness to obey, because to hear and not obey is an exercise in futility that will yield no positive results. Your word declares that your sheep know your voice. I pray that this book cause individuals to be sure that they are sheep in your fold and not sheep hanging around the outskirts of your fold because they have not yet accepted you as their personal Savior and therefore do not have the privilege of hearing you speak.

*Amen.*

# Prayer of Salvation

If you are not sure that you are one of God's sheep or that you are saved and you want Christ to come into your life, then pray this simple prayer:

Father, please forgive me of all of my sins and come into my life. I believe that you are God and your son, Jesus Christ, died for my sins that I might be saved. I believe that your son rose from the dead and has risen with all power in His hands. I want to be saved, please come into my heart, in Jesus' name! I thank you and I praise you for saving me.

*Amen.*

## The Book Cover

I began writing this book many years ago. When God first placed it in my heart, I knew what the title would be as well as the picture that would be on the cover. I had a vivid image of the book having a sky blue background with lightning streaming down from the letter "S" in the word speaks. While I didn't give much thought to the cover of the book, I knew that it should look just as I had imagined it in my mind.

As the years passed by, I saw so many authors write books which featured their pictures on the front covers. I had a fleeting thought that maybe I too should have a nice picture on the front of my book cover. But it was exactly that--a "fleeting thought." It came and left within a matter of seconds. I had already envisioned the picture that I believed God had given me for the cover. I also recognized that this book was not about me but it was a representation of the power of God and our ability to discern, and obey His voice.

As time went on, God began to speak to me about the significance of the book cover and how it relates to God's voice. The cover features lightning because lightning is quick, and powerful. It has a way of stopping us in our tracks and getting our attention in such a way that causes us to acknowledge that there must be a God somewhere. Most people would rather not walk or drive when there is thundering and lightning. If we are able to sit still and wait until the storm passes, we will do so because we realize that lightning can wreak a lot of havoc and has proven to be deadly at times.

The word of God and the voice of God can be just like lightning—quick and powerful. It definitely grabs our attention. When God speaks a powerful word of revelation where He is offering wisdom or instructions to us audibly, within our spirits, in a dream or vision, through the preached word, or through the Logos or Rhema word, it is always memorable. It is also relevant, timely, and significant and it often will give us a whole new direction or perspective about a person, thing, or situation. The revelation that God gives us is outside of the realm of our own thinking; therefore, we know that this truth embraced with the peacefulness of God had to come from God Himself.

Made in the USA
Middletown, DE
11 April 2016